UNF*CK YOUR BUSINESS FINANCES

UNF*CK YOUR BUSINESS FINANCES

Unlearn the Shame,
Reclaim the Power
and Change the Game

LAURA LINDEN

First published in Great Britain in 2025
by Authors & Co.
www.authorsandco.pub

ISBN 978-1-917623-20-9 (paperback)
ISBN 978-1-917623-21-6 (hardback)

To every woman who has ever been told to 'stay in her lane'. May this book help you own the whole f*cking road.

CONTENTS

PREFACE

The gender gap in financial literacy is huge.

And it pisses me off.

If you've ever wanted to learn about money but believe you aren't smart enough, worthy enough, or even allowed to have this knowledge, this book is for you. It won't teach you how to become an accountant or how to hack a spreadsheet. That's not the goal here. The goal is to help you learn just enough about your numbers to ask the right questions, use them to your advantage and take control of your wealth. When you do that, it can change everything for you.

In this book, I speak directly to women and the cis-female experience, not because men don't need financial education – there are men out there who do, of course – but because I know what it's like to live and work in this world as a woman. Through writing this book, however, I have come to realise it isn't just for women. It is for anyone who does not fit into the stereotype of what a typical business owner or entrepreneur looks or sounds like. It is for the person from a financially marginalised or underrepresented minority with the skill and talent to build the wealth they deserve, but without the confidence, privilege or opportunity to be taught. Financial literacy isn't solely about money. It is about freedom. And it's about time more women, minorities and marginalised people had it in their hands.

I want to be clear that this book is not anti-men. I love men. I love their company, I love their humour, and I have built wonderful working relationships with many men. I don't offend easily and have a grotesque sense of humour.

This book is anti-bullshit.

I spent over a decade in male-dominated companies, showing them the best way to use money, working hard to fit into that world. I learned early on that to be taken seriously, I had to become one of the 'lads'. Join in with the banter and play down my 'female-ness'.

I infiltrated the boys' club and was allowed to learn all their secrets. I thought I'd cracked it.

Then, during a career break after having my first child, things began to shift. I took on consultancy work for entrepreneurs and small businesses. I knew I wanted to return to work eventually, and consultancy would help me avoid a massive gap in my work history. But I quickly realised I had no idea about the real financial struggles of small business owners.

Most of the business owners I worked with – who, as with my former corporate colleagues, were predominately male – couldn't afford full-time finance help, so they ended up making a hash of it themselves (or getting their wives to help.) Even when the female business owners and wives of male business owners were good at numbers, they were still lost when it came to business finances and the nuances that come with managing money. This lack of financial experience was preventing these businesses, and the women working with them, from reaching the success I knew they could achieve.

I thought that was just how things were. I had worked with and been part of networks of women, all starting their own small businesses. I already knew that unless they had trained in accountancy or law, most were utterly lost when it came to their finances. But I didn't question it. Apart from offering advice occasionally, what more could I do?

Then, in 2013, I was forced to look at the world through my daughter's eyes.

My daughter is fearless, sharp and creative. She loves music: she sings and plays instruments. She also plays football, rugby and cricket; she absolutely nails people twice her size on the rugby pitch.

When the time came for her to move from junior school to senior school, we started looking for schools that offered rugby as a core sport, but quickly hit a problem. We could not find a single senior school that offered girls' rugby as a core sport. In her junior school, girls were allowed to play rugby with boys. But in senior school, co-ed rugby is not allowed. They legally have to have separate teams.

If she wanted to keep playing the sport she loved – and was bloody good at – we'd have to find a way to pay for it at the weekends while the boys got to continue it as part of their everyday education. The only options were netball or hockey: sports she hated. Her love of sport, and all the wonderful, beautiful things that come with that, was going to disappear because no school was equipped to support her.

How was that fair? I had no explanation or solution for her.

I tried telling her, "Maybe it's just not a traditional girls' sport."

"But if they offered it, wouldn't more girls play? Then it would become a girls' sport, right?" she asked.

She was right, of course, and the unfairness and inequity of it all filled me with rage. **Why did she have to change and make compromises just because the system wasn't equipped to support her?**

This is exactly what happens with women and money.

We tell women they don't belong in certain spaces, and then we act surprised when they don't show up. We don't design systems or spaces that support them, and then we wonder why they struggle to succeed.

I had seen misogyny at play in companies I worked with, but I hadn't done anything to help. And now my daughter was on the first step towards experiencing that same world. The realisation filled me with guilt and regret.

It was all very well, me saying to her, "Don't change who you are. Be this feisty little lunatic that you are, and don't give up," but I hadn't done the same. I had spent years trying to crowbar myself into being a different person just so I could fit into these male-dominated environments. But how did that help anyone else? I still regret that I wasted all that time being someone I'm not, simply because the space wasn't designed with me in mind.

That is why this book matters.

I don't want my daughter to grow up in a world where she has to be something she's not. Where doors slam in her face just because she's a girl. I need to do something about it.

I know I won't change everything overnight. But if one woman reads this book and realises she *can* understand her finances, she *can* build a massive, beautiful, wonderful business; she *can* build wealth, then I'll be delighted: I'll have done something. Because when women have more money, every person benefits. And you'll realise how much as you read this book.

We currently live in a bullshit system that doesn't just hurt women, it hurts men too. It teaches them that they can't be anything but providers, no matter what the cost to their mental health and relationships. It is unbalanced and unfair. We need to spread the burden of financial income and help each other. Providing is bloody hard work, and men shouldn't have to shoulder it alone, in the same way that women shouldn't have to shoulder the caregiving alone. There is no balance in one person being the designated breadwinner and the other the caregiver. If we can rebalance it, or at least shrink the gap a bit, that's got to benefit everyone, hasn't it?

When everyone is on the same level, it alleviates the burden on both sides. When women understand money, families can share the entire load. Not just finances, but caregiving too. When couples share knowledge and responsibilities, it can build trust and reduce the division that comes from each not understanding the burden the other experiences.

That's why we need to remove the gatekeepers and give all this knowledge to anyone who wants it, not just those who can afford to pay for it. If you agree that financial literacy can benefit all people, then this book is for you.

So, fuck the guilt and regret. (Maybe keep a little of the rage.) And let's start.

READ THIS FIRST

Imagine you've started a business doing what you love. You are creative. Ambitious. You have some bloody great ideas. You know there's more to life than what you've been given, and you're determined not to spend the rest of it regretting you never took a chance.

So, you start.

Soon, you begin to experience the late nights and painfully early mornings. Your friends support you, but they also think you're mad. You miss your children. Your partner begins to feel like a stranger. But you keep going. You know that if you can get your business to the point where it's running well on its own or is valuable enough to sell, it will all be worth it.

It *will* pay off.

Then, one day, you realise something is missing from your business – what is it?

You need more. More insight to make better and more *profitable* decisions.

Maybe you're ready to find an investor and the credibility and clout it would bring.

But your strengths aren't in maths or finance, so you start to ask around. And you hear the horror stories of other female founders feeling intimidated or dismissed in meetings. You watch a bit too much *Dragons' Den* and cringe as business owners fail to answer questions about their finances. With less than 1%[1] of investment going to female-founded businesses, your confidence wobbles. Can you really do this? Was all that hard work for nothing?

I see it all the time: lots of wonderful women with great business ideas who get stuck. We can't get funding or we don't have enough financial knowledge to take our business to the next stage.

Many women aren't given the financial awareness and experience they deserve. Countless unseen variables and biases too entrenched for this book mean society is structured in such a way that women are less likely to have access to financial education or the 'right' networks, and therefore do not receive the financial opportunities they deserve.

Intelligent, ambitious women aren't given a seat at the table, are left out of boardrooms and C-suites, and as a result, the glass ceiling keeps getting higher and higher.

Why You Shouldn't Give Up

In 2018, McKinsey & Co.[2] conducted research into female entrepreneurship in the UK. They found that **£250 billion** could be added to the UK's economy if women were supported and financed to build businesses at the same rate as men.

Ok, but what does this really mean?

When there are more female-led businesses, there are more women with financial power. When more women are in decision-making[3] roles, we (at a societal, political level) are more likely to make policies and decisions that benefit women, children and families. More women with financial power means more women with the ability, tools and freedom to make decisions that impact *everyone* for the better.

At a local level, it means:

- More businesses with more jobs on offer.
- More *flexible* jobs built around how women live and work. (As women, we are more likely to be responsible for childcare and elderly care *in addition* to our careers. [4] We also have more demands on our health, such as pregnancy, menopause and menstruation.)
- Better wages and more flexibility mean people can spend more locally, boosting local communities.
- More funding from tax revenues means better schools, healthcare and transport.
- More local shops and businesses increase competition and drive down prices.

If more women built businesses that made as much money as men's, we could fundamentally change the world.

However, this is not about competing with men. This is not about going to war with them. This is about promoting financial harmony and equality between us, so it can benefit *all* our personal lives. When women have financial independence and power, there are more opportunities and choices for women *and* men. When there is financial equality, men and women can share financial responsibilities, and as part of that, the burden of understanding the numbers. They can both choose paths that fulfil them, and if that means there are more stay-at-home dads and career women, that's great. Men shouldn't always have to carry the burden of being the sole 'provider'.

When my family and I lived in Dubai, I heard of so many men who got into awful debt, and their wives knew nothing about it because they were too ashamed to tell them. Some ended up in jail, and some took their own lives. Surely, if we shared the financial burden equally as well as the parenting burden, we would all have more balanced, healthy lives. Men wouldn't feel ashamed of seeking help or that taking their own lives was the only answer to problems. Boys could grow up seeing equality from a young age and not feel threatened by it. Women rising up should not automatically mean men fail, like some financial seesaw.

For some reason, it hasn't happened.

Yet.

If we want change, we need more women with successful businesses. More women with hundreds of thousands, if not millions, in the bank, and female-led businesses receiving investment. Because even with brilliant initiatives like Female Invest and Female Founders Rise, or the industry-led, government-backed Invest in Women Taskforce,[5] women still need to know *how to manage their money once they get it*.

There are a million people telling women how to make money and helping us to get it. Nobody is telling us how to *keep* it.

What do we do once we have that money?

What do the numbers all mean, and how do we manage them for profit?

What This Book Will Do for You

You will be relieved to know I am not going to teach you how to become an accountant. This is not an accounting textbook.

But you need to understand as much as you can about your numbers in order to discover the best way to grow a profitable and resilient business so that, in turn, you can build your own personal wealth. After all, what is a business? It is a money-*making* asset. If it's not making money, and you're not getting anything out of it, it's not an asset. Money is essential, like the foundations of a house. You need it; without it, the whole thing crumbles. But nobody will sit there and tell you what you need to know about running your business, because it's *your* business.

Therefore, *you* should be the first person to understand those numbers.

My hope is that after you read this book, your fear and uncertainty around your finances will be gone, and that you will be able to look at your cash flow or your balance sheet and know if you can afford to relax a little or if you need to push harder. People tend to bury their heads and think, "I'll just deal with an issue when it comes." But if you plan for an issue and see it coming, that problem would never arrive. Think of it like learning to read the weather and figuring out what the signs are telling you. Dark clouds in the sky most likely mean rain, maybe a storm. You can choose to stay inside that day or go out with your wellies. If it's sunny, you know it's a good day to water the garden and jet wash the patio. We all successfully manage our lives around the seasons and changing weather. We can't predict everything, but we know how to read the signs and prepare for the most likely outcome.

It is the same with your finances. And this book will show you how to do that.

What You Will Learn

By the end of this book, you'll know how best to build a resilient, profitable business. You will know:

- Exactly when you're going to run out of cash.
- If you're growing too quickly.
- If you're hiring correctly.
- If you're in the right market.
- If you're spending too much on marketing.
- Which revenue streams to focus on.
- When to start thinking about investment.
- How much profit you can and should make.
- What to do with surplus cash.
- When and how to pay yourself.
- When to buy stock and assets.
- How much you should spend on office costs.
- How to remunerate your staff.

- How to incentivise your team and keep them for the long game.
- How and when to sell your business.
- How to compare your business to competitors.
- How to budget and forecast.
- Policies and processes to keep things efficient.
- How and when to get funding.
- And what the hell your accountant is talking about!

Part 1: Foundations

We will cover the foundations first: why you shouldn't worry about maths and how to think about money. You will identify which of three types of business you're building because each type requires you to follow a particular path to success. From local coffee shops to massive international brand empires, businesses generally fall into one of these three categories. I will introduce them, and you can discover which path you're on in Chapter 3.

Between 2011 and the time of writing this book, I worked with three companies as a CFO: one was a 'Lifestyle' business, one was a 'Legacy' business, and one was a business that, with my help, was ultimately sold for a very large sum of money. I will share their stories with you because they represent the three main types of businesses that exist today. Their names have been changed to maintain confidentiality, but they are real former clients of mine.

Part 2: Keep Your Money

This will introduce the financial essentials: profit and loss, balance sheets, and cash. In other words, it tells you how to *keep* what you earn. This is the financial knowledge most people need but have never been taught, so be prepared to focus. Once you understand these essentials, everything else will begin to fall into place.

Part 3: Grow Your Money

In this part, we'll cover ways to make your money work for you. That means budgeting and forecasting, systems, KPIs and taxes. (I'll share some things you didn't know you needed to know.) All are essential for a business that will make you profitable. Most people reading financial books, even accountants, tend to fall asleep at this point. But please bear with me. I promise it'll be worth it because Part 3 is how you turn the money you *have* into the money you *dream of having*.

Part 4: Money x People = Profit

On to my mission: getting more funding for you. This part will cover funding, investors and incentive schemes. I won't teach you how to get funding; that's not my expertise, but I can prepare you for what investors look for and how best to prepare your numbers and decks. I will also talk to you about building teams and working with accountants. Money and people are closely connected, and you need to know how to work with the best people to give you the best profit.

At the end of most of the chapters in this book, I've included a 'Think Like a CFO' exercise. These are exercises based on what I would do if I were managing a business's finances. They are not essential, but I recommend trying them so you start to feel confident managing your finances. If you feel you'd like to learn more or you're curious about diving deeper, you can download the Feisty FD app or reach out to enquire about working with me one-to-one. Scan the QR code below for more information.

The book will end by covering how not to fuck it up when things go well. Don't skip to this part until you've read the earlier parts. I know 'How not to fuck it up' is a great chapter heading, but you won't understand a thing unless you've read everything else.

Why You Should Read This Book

This is the stuff that will help you sleep at night. If you're going to embark on this journey, you need to know this shit. I promise you that numbers are nothing to fear, because – and this is the secret no one wants you to know – accounting and finance in business have nothing at all to do with maths.

Yes, really.

I am crap at maths. Absolutely dreadful. I can't do mental arithmetic, so don't ask me to. But give me a spreadsheet and I can work magic. I can help you make a ton of money. When you know how to run a business the *right* way, you won't have to work as hard; you won't have to outrun everything, and you won't run the risk of selling your soul to make money when the cracks start to show, because you'll know how to stop the cracks from appearing in the first place. You can be confident that the decisions you make are the right ones.

When you get this right, you can go off and live the life you want, whether that's buying a bigger house, going on more holidays, giving back to other people or just having more security. It all starts here.

Have No Regrets

Part of my role as a CFO is to help companies improve their finances so they can sell the business for a profit, if that's their goal. If the sale goes particularly well, I get a bonus. But after one particular business sold, I realised I hadn't asked for a bonus that I believed reflected what I deserved.

I was pissed off.

Other people got way more than me and I should have asked for more. And I *could* have asked for more because if I had, I probably would have got more. I'd worked for it.

But I hadn't.

I don't want anyone to miss out on the money they deserve simply for not asking the right questions. When you arm yourself with the knowledge and confidence to ask for what you deserve, you have the tools to make the impact you want.

Anyone can learn how to read numbers. Anyone can build a business that is profitable and resilient and that gives them what they want.

You are one of those people.

PART 1

FOUNDATIONS

1

WHY YOU DON'T NEED TO BE GOOD AT MATHS TO MAKE MONEY

How many times have you looked at your business numbers and thought, *What the fuck is that trying to tell me?* Flashback to awkward maths lessons where you're feeling confused and lost in class, convinced you'll never understand numbers. *Why bother trying?*

You're not alone.

Numbers feel scary, especially money numbers. They're complicated and confusing. It doesn't help that no one teaches us this stuff. So, when you get your first paycheck, what do you do? Most people piss it up the wall and get into trouble. Our relationships with money are steeped in shame and silence. We are all so embarrassed about getting into debt or not understanding our accounts, but how would you ever know unless your school gave classes on it or your parents sat you down to talk about it?

A stigma develops around money. Whatever our upbringing, we believe it's either boring, unsexy, stressful or for other people to worry about. No one wants to think about money. Why would you? You can deal with it later. Just do the bare minimum to get by. Who wants to think about chasing invoices or navigating complex Purchase

Order systems when you could be focusing on your passion? Earning money or building your business is a lot more fun. As long as you're bringing in money, that stuff will sort itself out, right?

But what happens when HMRC comes knocking? You think you're safe with £200,000 in the bank, but you still don't have enough money to pay your bill. (That actually happened to a client before they hired me.) A lot of entrepreneurs can be on top of their invoices and are profitable on paper, but somehow, they have no cash in the bank to pay their staff. When you bury your head in the sand or assume someone else will fix the numbers for you, you will never build a business that gives you the money or freedom you want. Decisions based on human error are when things start to go very wrong. Not just in your finances but in your leadership, your staff, marketing, sales: everything. You need insight into your numbers to know what is working and what isn't. That way, you can make informed decisions about how to build your business the *right* way. In other words, you can operate in the most efficient way possible so there is as little room as possible for human error.

Why Can't I Just Get an Accountant?

It is reasonable to think that the solution to your finances is just to hire an accountant. They will tell you what you need to know, right?

Not necessarily.

An accountant gets in, does the job and gets out. It is the complete luck of the draw as to whether you get someone who **actually** gives a shit about your business and tells you exactly what you need to know. They won't know enough about your business to know what to tell you. They might not care either. They won't tell you if you need to spend less on staff and more on processes. They won't think to tell you if your margins are so tight that you won't be able to sell for the number you want. They might see that you're overspending and you'll be broke in three months, but will they feel comfortable enough to tell you – the boss? Unless you tell them that's what you're looking for, they won't give you the information you need.

The problem is that most people don't know what they need to know.

When you're starting up a business, you do *all* the jobs: accounting, HR, ops, sales and marketing. When you do everything, you forget things or don't prioritise them correctly. That's not a big problem today, but let's say you forget to send an invoice. Payments get delayed. Suppliers don't get paid on time. Rent can get missed. Suddenly, it's been three months, and you can't pay your staff. Your suppliers refuse to deliver unless you pay their bill. Your business does not look good, you struggle to sleep, and you begin to make bad decisions.

On the other hand, being extremely busy means you could be overly cautious with your money, and you do something you wouldn't even think is inefficient, like paying your invoices early.

Yes, that's inefficient.

If you'd left that money in your bank until your invoice's deadline, you could have made a bit of extra cash thanks to the interest on your account. This is not a big problem, but when you think about it, over time, you could have made a good amount of money with very little effort.

All my clients have made mistakes in one way or another. It isn't that you're bad with numbers or that your accountant is crap, it's that without realising it, we create tiny inefficiencies and overlook details that can add up to big problems. Don't build a house on weak foundations; cracks will appear that will cost you later. It is better to build strong foundations first.

The Foundations

Earlier, I wrote about the money problems a business owner might have. Did you notice that all those problems have a common characteristic?

It's not a trick question.

There is one thing most business issues have in common:

None of them has anything to do with maths and everything to do with operations.

When you think about business 'operations', what instantly comes to mind?

Daily processes. Company targets. Perhaps it's the way you manage your staff or file your paperwork. (It is also okay if your mind goes blank at this point and you have no idea what I'm talking about.)

Operations is how you *operate*, right?

Your operations are the day-to-day tasks that keep your business running. If we were to compare this to regular life, it'd be how you decide to split dinner between you, your partner and your kids. It would be how high you turn the heating versus putting your socks on. Choosing to shop at Aldi or Waitrose. Buying more fuel to put in the car versus walking.

When I lived and worked in Dubai, I drove my children to school every weekday morning, still dressed in my dog-walking shorts, with poo bags in my pockets and unbrushed hair. All the other mothers stood at the school gates, beautiful and pristine.

One morning, I turned to my husband in frustration after facing these catwalk-ready mothers yet again, and I said, "If I woke up at 5 am, and I still look like this, what time are they waking up?" Mark looked at me like it was the most obvious thing in the world. "They're waking up five minutes before they leave the house," he said. "They have a maid; they have a nanny; they have a driver. You're doing it all.'"

Operating efficiently is about how you choose to spend your time and money.

Those women chose to operate their lives in a far more efficient way than mine. Of course, how much money we can spend on outsourcing plays a huge role in what we can do, but that's what running a business is: resource planning; choosing how and where to put your time and money to get more bang for your buck. But many business owners don't think about running their business the same way we think about running our homes. We know the cost of turning the heating up in our houses, but we don't really know the cost of hiring too many people too quickly. It is easy to know if we can afford to splash out at Waitrose this month, but we aren't so sure if it's worth investing in a new Head of Sales.

In the world of business operations, business owners tend to treat money as something separate: a by-product, an afterthought or the reward you get for running the business.

That is the wrong way to think about it.

Instead, *how you operate* your business determines how much money you make. Let's take an example from one of my clients: I found £300 a month of pointless spending by simply going through their subscriptions and direct debits. I immediately cancelled them. That is £300 in their pocket every month that they didn't have before. It didn't matter if they had the best sales or marketing or a number one best-selling product; they were wasting money through bad internal operations, and they didn't know it. They can now use that money to make their business better. You can have the perfect business mindset, superstar sales and viral marketing, but if you don't **operate** correctly, none of that matters.

All those gag-inducing sayings you hear, like 'Work Smarter, Not Harder' are actually true. People get trapped believing that they're stuck with their business costs, so they've just got to make enough money to cover them. But they're not. You can tweak them and make your numbers better. You can negotiate things to mean that your cost base is lower, which means you don't have to work as hard, and more money goes into your pocket.

Why would you want to *have* to cover a grand's worth of costs before you see any of the money? If you could reduce that £1,000 of costs to £500 a month, that's less work you have to do and fewer clients you have to find.

Alternatively, that's an extra £500 in your pocket.

When you think smarter and more strategically about your money, it means more power to you. More money in your pocket and more money towards building a business that aligns with your values, or donating to charities you care about, or spending more time with your family.

It's about smart resource allocation.

It is about pie.

The Money Pie

Imagine a pie or a pizza. Choose your favourite. I choose a pie. Imagine that the pie represents your revenue. (Revenue is income you earn from selling your goods or services.)

All the effort that goes into making that pie is the work you put into your business: the blood, sweat, tears and stress. It is hard work, but you're proud of it and it's a bloody good pie.

Now you share that pie (revenue) with the people involved in your business:

- You give one slice to the people on your payroll.
- Another slice goes out for rent.
- Another slice goes to your suppliers.
- One goes in your pocket.

What is left is your profit.

Profit

Payroll

The Money Pie

Tax

Suppliers Rent

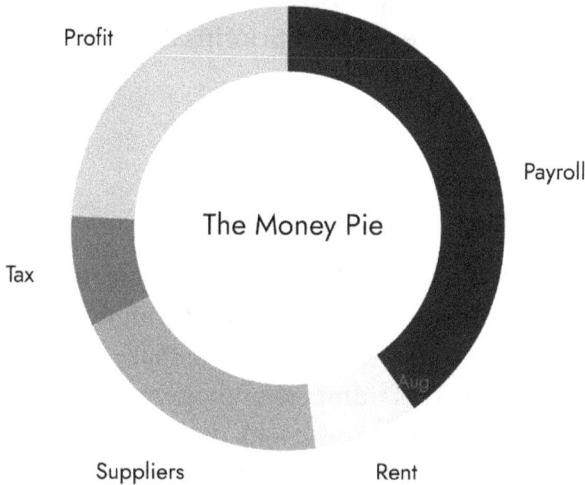

Think for a moment about *your* imaginary pie. (If you don't have a business pie yet, you can make one up or use your personal finances as an example.) Get out a pen and notepad and draw a circle. Then slice it up:

- How many slices are you giving away?
- How big or small are they?
- Are you happy with your slice? Could it be bigger?

This is about strategy and prioritising resources. You want to find ways to make your business pie more financially efficient so you get the rewards you want. The rewards don't always have to be more money; they could be more time, flexibility or recognition.

Most people think the answer is to make the pie bigger. But that means working harder for longer hours. Yes, you'll have a bigger pie (more money), but you'll have to give away more slices because to bake a bigger pie, there'll be more demands on your resources.

Why not make the pie smaller and give it to fewer people? Or give them less and keep more for yourself. And that's not a selfish thing. You can keep more for yourself and still be a good business owner. We will talk more about business mindset and motivations in Chapter 2.

For now, just know that improving your business operations means better planning and more efficient prioritisation of resources.

In our case, the resource of money.

One More Thing

Before we move on to the next chapter, it's important to set expectations. While I will give you as much information as I can about operating a profitable and resilient business, that's very different from putting it into action. This numbers and operations stuff is a whole new skill you have to learn, and it's ok if you find this hard. In fact, I give you permission to find this hard and boring and annoying.

Nothing you learned at school will have prepared you for entrepreneurship, unless you took Business Studies, but even then, when I studied that it didn't teach me anything about running a business. And as far as I know, Financial Literacy has never been part of the UK's school curriculum; no wonder there are generations of women (and men) who will struggle with money.

Even reading this chapter, I bet you already feel some resistance or anxiety, but you can't run a resilient and profitable business if you're not mentally prepared. That's why, in the next chapter, we will explore mindset and your relationship with money. This is the psychological side of the business. You can't make a shit ton of money if your relationship with money is flawed. Even though I'm nowhere near qualified enough to talk about business psychology or mental health, it is worth exploring your relationship with money, how you behave around it and how you treat it before we dive into the cool and sexy accounting stuff. It's all connected, and it all matters.

By the Way...

If you plan to get funding for your business, the list of shit you'll have to overcome is endless, not just mindset and limiting beliefs, but obstacles from other people too. Doors will be slammed left, right and centre, and a lot of those doors will have men standing behind them. I have experiences I can't share, but I want you to know that I've been left out of high-level conversations and had doors closed on me simply because I was a woman. That is not intended to scare you but to motivate you to do something about it. Be even *more* prepared and *more* determined to know your numbers so you can hold your own in that investor meeting.

Now You Know

To make money and run a profitable business:

1. You ***don't*** need to be good at maths, but you ***do*** need to have efficient business operations.
2. An accountant will not solve all your problems. You need to know the right questions to ask to make the right financial decisions for ***your*** business.
3. You need to strategise and prioritise your resources to get the results you want.

Luckily for you, we'll cover all of that in this book.

2

EVERYTHING YOU BELIEVE
ABOUT MONEY IS A LIE

Imagine being told at age four that playing with money is not something that girls do.

Then at age seven that only boys are good at maths.
At nine, girls shouldn't ask about money.
By twelve, imagine your father controlled any money you had.
At fifteen, you are told only men can be in charge of money.
At eighteen, your boyfriend or husband controls your money.
At twenty-one, when you get pregnant, your income disappears.

What would that do to you? What would you believe about yourself? And what would your relationship with money be like?

I bet it would mess with your head.

This was the reality for many of our mothers and grandmothers over the last fifty to one hundred years. Although things slowly changed in the first half of the twentieth century, it took until the mid-1970s and 1980s for things to improve significantly. Until then, women couldn't even open bank accounts without a signature from a father or husband. Unequal pay was legal, and maternity pay didn't exist. If you wanted to start a family, you had to find a rich husband because you'd be out of a job the minute you got pregnant.

Crap, right?

Even though our laws have changed, we are still dealing with the fallout of generations of women who have been excluded, controlled and silenced regarding money. According to The WealthiHer Network Report[6] men and women still tend to fall into certain financial roles: women take care of the daily domestic expenses while men do the long-term planning. Only 23% of women take charge of long-term financial planning decisions. This leaves many women completely unprepared to make financial decisions when their partners die, they divorce, or they find themselves as single parents. Even though women are more financially independent than they have been for centuries, we are still battling inherited beliefs around money:

- I should be grateful for what I have.
- Talking about money is rude.
- Men are better with money; I'll just make mistakes.
- I don't deserve money.
- I'm not clever enough to manage money.
- It's not my place to think about money.
- People will think I'm arrogant or greedy if I want money.
- I shouldn't try and change things, this is just how it is.
- Earning money isn't my job.
- I'll just marry a rich man.

These beliefs don't just hold us back, they affect the way we earn money, spend it, save, invest, and manage our wealth.

That's a big problem. Because something big is coming, and we are not ready.

The Great Wealth Transfer

At the time of writing, women control 32%[7] of global wealth: approximately $72 trillion. By 2030, women in the European Union and the US are expected to own up to 45% of financial assets.[8]

This is thanks to a massive financial shift called The Great Wealth Transfer, a forecasted wealth 'hand-off' of about $84.4 trillion[9] from Baby Boomers and the Silent Generation to the younger generation.

Assets. Stocks. Businesses. Fortunes. Cars. Real Estate. All changing hands.

And because women outlive men and are becoming more financially independent, a huge share of that is going to be managed by women. Whether we are ready or not, women are becoming the primary financial decision-makers, and it's being called 'the power shift of the century'.[10]

But if women have never been taught to manage money, what will happen to that wealth?

The financial sector has historically been geared towards men. Advisors still consider men to be the main financial decision makers in heterosexual couples, often neglecting to build professional relationships with women. This sector often overlooks younger women, and a lack of diverse teams means women are less likely to feel confident finding someone they feel comfortable talking to.

Ultimately, women are not fully seen or understood by wealth managers or investors, and this lack of open conversation around money has created an intergenerational financial gap.

The biggest misconception we have to deal with is the assumption that financially independent women have the same goals as men and behave the same way as men. We don't behave the same way as men, generally. Why then would we choose to act as men when it comes to our money? Research by McKinsey has found that women have unique behaviours and preferences when it comes to money, such as preferring to make financial decisions based on our values. We are more risk-averse and we prefer in-person financial advice and personalised support. Women take a more measured and cautious approach to investing and tend to focus on achieving specific goals rather than reaping the highest returns.

I once spoke to a wealth advisor because I wanted specific advice about educational trusts, but he spent the entire time telling me why I should be preparing for retirement. Why? I didn't ask for that information. I was not there for retirement planning advice. If I, as a CFO, still don't get the financial advice I ask for, or that aligns with my specific financial goals, what hope do women have who *aren't* financially literate?

All of this tells me that it's more important than ever for us to learn about money and to work on our money mindset. Women are not the same as men when it comes to money, and we should not be pushed into investing as a man would. We should be able to hold our own in conversations with financial experts who may, whether they intend to or not, come across as intimidating.

But that's easier said than done.

We all have money hangups and limiting beliefs, but when it's such a huge part of our futures, we *have* to address them. Numbers give us control over our personal and business finances, so we *have* to change the way we think about them.

Between 2018 and 2023, the percentage of European women who feel 'somewhat comfortable' or 'totally comfortable' making financial decisions rose from approximately 45% to 67% with millennial women leading the way.[11] That is bloody brilliant.

But there is more we can do. We should make sure we learn everything we can about money so we can hold on to it, and that includes learning about ourselves. (Yes, we're getting a bit woo-woo.)

I'm not a psychologist, but I am a finance expert, and from where I'm sitting, there are certain inherited beliefs around money and numbers that always get in the way. So let's talk about them before we move any further. What I'm about to teach you in this book isn't going to help if you aren't aware of what could be holding you back.

Inherited Beliefs That Need To Eff Off

Inherited Belief 1:
You Are Not Smart Enough

There is always someone who told us we were dumb or that we weren't good at maths. There is always a comment that just sticks, such as, "Oh God, you're so bad with money." 57%[12] of women defer to their partners in important financial decisions, saying, "My spouse never encouraged me," or, "My spouse knows more," as an excuse. But that stuff really pisses me off. I'm sure you battle with those beliefs every day, but how true are those things you tell yourself? Are they things someone else told you because they were bad with money?

Most of us have a money mindset that could do with a little tweaking. But no matter how crap you *think* you are with money, you *do* have a basic understanding of it: you know that you get money in and it goes back out again. You choose what that money is spent on, and you know how to get money. No matter how financially illiterate you are, or *think* you are, you do have that basic understanding, and that's enough to start with.

I don't believe that being good with money is equal to being 'clever'. My daughter sings, plays the guitar and the cello and is learning to play the drums. She can read four different types of sheet music – and she thinks she's stupid because she doesn't do well at maths. Is she right? My son is what most people would call 'clever'. He has an extraordinary memory and is naturally academically gifted. But does that mean he will naturally be good with money? As you learned in the last chapter, being good with money isn't about being good at maths. School teaches us that what matters is being 'smart', which means having good grades. But how does that translate into the real world, after school?

People think accountants are clever because we deal with money all the time. Are we? (We're not.) We have just learned a set of rules, and we know how to follow them. That's it. I am crap at maths, but I am fucking brilliant with data and business logistics, and here I am helping businesses exit with millions of pounds. Don't you dare see yourself as less than anyone else just because you don't tick the 'academic' box. If no one ever sat you down and taught you about money, of course you'll struggle. A lack of knowledge in one area does not mean you are inherently dumb. It just means you have gaps in your education.

My son, who is naturally academic but bores easily, doesn't thrive in a normal school environment because it isn't challenging enough for him: even the gifted ones have gaps. So we've got to fill those spaces ourselves. There are more and more people who don't fit into that box of being academic, who don't do well in exams, but who have found things that fit their personality and passions, and they've just flown. To be good with money, all you need is curiosity and a willingness to learn; it shows self-awareness and a desire to improve. Those are signs of an intelligent and capable person.

Inherited Belief 2:
Money Makes You a Bad Person

Everyone has a stigma around money they've gained from their parents, their upbringing, school or their environment. When I was younger, I believed talking about money was crass and wealthy people were arrogant, brash and snobby. No one taught me this; I created it in my head after watching my mother, who came from a disadvantaged background, feel uncomfortable at parties with her wealthy friends.

You might have received the message that money is dirty, that it turns you into a Mr. Burns character from *The Simpsons* who hates everyone, and that you'd end up lonely because everyone would just want you for your money. It is hard to shake off those beliefs, and obviously, no one wants to be called arrogant or selfish. But if you want to build a successful and profitable business, you have to be okay with earning and spending money. Work on your negative associations with money because if deep down you think money is bad, you will never make any. Your business will never be profitable. You will find ways to lose money, consciously or unconsciously.

I know it's never going to be okay that there are people worse off than you. We are not saving lives here, and the people who do probably earn a tenth of what they truly deserve. And that's shit. But you not going after what you want isn't going to change that. If that's something that bothers you, build a business that changes things for the better. Earn so much money that you can donate everything to the charity that means the most to you or that changes the system.

MacKenzie Scott is a billionaire who was ranked the ninth most powerful woman in the world by Forbes in 2024.[13] After divorcing Jeff Bezos in 2019, she signed the Giving Pledge, promising to give away at least half of her wealth over the course of her lifetime.[14] According to Yield Giving, the philanthropic foundation she established in 2020 to share her financial fortune, she has donated $19.3bn (£15.5bn) to more than 2,450 nonprofits so far.

Laurene Powell Jobs is committed to distributing her wealth 'in ways that lift up individuals and communities in a sustainable way'.[15] She is especially focused on mitigating climate change, and in 2021 pledged to donate $3.5bn (£2.8bn) through her nonprofit Waverley Street Foundation.

Having money does not mean you're a bad person. What you do with it and how you use it reflects who you are.

Inherited Belief 3:
We Shouldn't Talk About Money

Absolute crap. It's a stupid belief, but a big one that a lot of us have. All it does is make the topic of money taboo and education inaccessible for the people who need it. We are all scared to ask questions or to admit we don't know about money, because we have been taught that it's bad manners or it's not our place to ask. So, we only talk about wins and successes: everyone paints their best life on social media. But not talking about money is a form of gate-keeping financial education that keeps people in the dark.

We should talk about our money issues in the same way as we encourage each other to talk about our mental health in order to support each other. If we talked about it, we could share the burden and feel more in control. We would feel less alone and less awkward about our money. Better financial education and a healthy relationship with money will only become available to those who need it if we start talking about money more.

Let's get rid of this belief that money talk is off-limits. Talk about it and figure out how it works. It is the only way to gain control over our futures. It is ok not to know everything about money, but it doesn't make sense to ignore it and hope it'll figure itself out. This book is a good place to start.

Inherited Belief 4:
You Should Be Grateful for What You Have

If you earn more, it does not mean someone else gets less. If you start a business, you're not taking someone else's wealth. If you get more money by generating more value through your business, you're boosting the economy, paying more tax, and spending more in your local area. You create opportunities for other businesses by buying from them. You make your wealth available to others by using it to support others. Obviously, there are exceptions to the rule, and some people squirrel it away. But most good people use it to help their friends and family, and their economy.

Gratitude is important. Whether you journal, pray or meditate, we are all encouraged to focus on being grateful for what we have. However, that often means we feel guilty and ashamed if we want more. At times, I've thought, "I'm in a really well-paid job. There are people who don't have jobs who would kill for mine. How selfish of me is it that I want more?" I have to kick myself and remind myself that I'm not asking for something for nothing, just for **different**. However, it's frowned upon, particularly for women, to say, "I want to be fucking loaded. I want to have a massive house, and I want to go and shop freely whenever I want," because it's seen as shallow or greedy. It is the whole Robin Hood story: rich people are rich because they take from the poor. You wanting more doesn't mean you're taking away from someone else; that's not how money works anymore. It's just bollocks.

You can be grateful for what you have and want more. I do.

Inherited Belief 5:
You Will Make Mistakes With Money

We all know there is a lack of female representation in leadership. It is not down to a lack of ability but to a lack of confidence and a fear of failure. 58%[16] of UK adults say that fear of failure is stopping them from starting businesses, with women more likely to use that as a reason not to try. But when making mistakes is as much an **inevitable** part of business as corporation tax or sales, you can't avoid it. You have to accept it as part of the whole system and not as a reflection of your value as a person because, let's be honest, we've all done stuff that's made us look stupid, haven't we? We've all whacked the baby's head on the car when trying to manoeuvre them into the seat, or forgotten to bring a spare nappy to soft play and been absolutely mortified to have to ask another mum. We've all tripped over a pothole, caught our finger in the door, or slipped on the dance floor. Said a stupid thing in a meeting. Forgot to file the tax returns. I pressed the wrong number on the keyboard and accidentally paid the wrong person a five-figure bonus once. Shit happens.

My kids' school teaches them that 'Fail' means First Attempt In Learning. And I love it. It is cheesy but so accurate. As a perfectionist, I hate failure, but it's how we learn. As an entrepreneur and business owner, you've got to get used to getting things wrong and not being perfect all the time. The quicker you realise what you're doing wrong, the quicker you can correct it. Better to mess it up quickly rather than slowly over the course of six months, by which point, you've wasted a lot of time and money. Don't make the mistake of believing it's proof of your inability to succeed. It is proof that you need to redirect your attention, and we'll cover this a lot more in Chapter 9.

Inherited Belief 6:
You Are Not Important Enough

Imagine you are in a room full of strangers. Every one of those people will be an expert at something, and so will you. Ask yourself, what are you the expert on? What do people come to you and ask for advice on? It doesn't matter if it's how to make the perfect pastry to go on a pie or how to gain 20% on the stock exchange.

I know a woman who had been an end-of-life doula for years. She knew how to help families through the grieving process and make the most of those last days with their loved ones. Most people might think, "How is that a business?" But now she has turned it into a business, she's making millions because she's giving value to people who need it. You have something in your head that someone else will pay you money for. Don't hold yourself back because you don't think it's big enough or valuable enough, or you think business is all about products and services.

For a long time, the thought that I had to be different and special to start my own business was a big obstacle for me. But you don't have to be special. There doesn't even need to be a reason for you to start. You just have to care about something and want something for yourself. The economy is missing out on what women could produce for it. We're missing out on the ideas that are in our heads: our life experiences, our passions and our solutions. It doesn't matter what they are. There is no less tangible value to it just because it came from you, whether it's how to change a nappy or how to solve world hunger, we're missing out on that knowledge. Don't stop yourself because you think it's not important enough. There are people out there who will think the opposite.

Inherited Belief 7:
You Have to Be Someone You're Not

To fit into male-dominated financial spaces, women often feel the pressure to squash their feminine characteristics and lean into more masculine ones. When I worked with large organisations, I played 'Corporate Laura'. If the space was very male-dominated, I would swear more and be more aggressive. It wasn't a conscious decision but influenced by the era I grew up in, the whole 'ladette' culture that was popular in the nineties. However, I was still squashing other parts of my personality, in particular the emotional stuff. I would bite my tongue a lot, and I wasn't as brave as I probably should or could have been. I didn't always speak up and say what I think. (That could also be my introverted nature, rather than being a woman.) It all helped me to adapt and survive in my workplace.

However, I was talking about this with a friend, and he made a good point: if we're trying to create diverse boardrooms and businesses, what's the point of having a woman there who is just going to act like another man? Doesn't that negate the entire point of diversity in the room? If she is going to act like another bloke, what's the point?

To create more space for women, for our ideas and our viewpoints, we need to show up exactly as we are without squashing any of those characteristics we fear make us appear 'too soft' or 'too bossy'. If you are naturally quite aggressive, I would argue that you shouldn't hide that. If you are an emotional woman, embrace that too. If we have to pretend to be someone else in business, we are in the wrong business. There are plenty of spaces where you can be exactly as you are; whether you're conservative and strait-laced or the complete opposite, there are environments that suit you. It is hard work being someone you're not, so don't work in an environment that doesn't allow you to be who you are. What's the point? If we want to change the dynamic of business and money, we've got to give ourselves permission to be authentically ourselves, whether that's emotional, assertive, curious, pedantic, nurturing or foul-mouthed. Otherwise, we just bring in more copies of what's already there... and look how well that's worked for everyone. The whole point of diversity is to have people with different experiences from different backgrounds. Not just to fill a chair or tick a box, but to have them bring those diverse experiences and ideas into the room for the benefit of the business. Otherwise, it absolutely negates the diversity we are working hard for.

A Message for Mothers

I have this really amazing friend who is one of the most genuine, kind, lovely people you'll ever meet. Her in-laws are incredibly successful and cerebral, with impressive jobs at well-known organisations. But she always says to me that she feels like a complete dumbass when she sits with them because she used to work in finance but doesn't anymore. She doesn't recognise her successes outside of the boardroom: raising three children, one of whom was born with and survived cancer; caring for her dad, dying really young; taking her mother to live with her. Just because she's not sitting in a boardroom at JP Morgan, why does that devalue her worth?

Many women in the world who have given up their careers to become mothers think, "What do I have to offer?" I know this because I've experienced it and discussed it with friends. It annoys me when women don't see the value of their experiences outside of work.

While raising children is seen as valuable, we often don't see the planning and work related to parenting as equally valuable. We might go from university or a job to motherhood without having a frigging clue how to cook, sew, manage diaries, cope with late nights, process big emotions or raise another human being. But we have all learned. You are not *just* changing nappies or *just* potty training; you're teaching a child how to pee, and that's not exactly a small task. You are not just planning a week's activities; you're managing the early development and emotional well-being of a child. If you've ever sold your kid's old clothes on Vinted, you mightn't think it takes a business mind to do it, but organising photos, pricing and competition analysis is something business owners do.

My husband, who works in Talent Acquisition, calls all this potential 'School Yard' talent: skill and knowledge often only found at the school gates, because the corporate world wasn't built for parents and doesn't fit with their roles. Their skills and potential aren't valued. These experiences are underappreciated and undervalued, which reduces our confidence in our skills and contributions. However, don't underestimate what you could offer just because you're not at a desk. We have all learned new skills, and we all have something to offer.

Trust Yourself

How can we break these negative beliefs and habits that are holding us back?

What I always do, and what I advise my clients to do, is to be prepared. A lot of the time when people fear the unknown, the advice they get is: 'Just do it scared.' And while I agree with that, I'd say, "Do it *prepared* and scared." Knowledge gives you power. So, arm yourself with as much financial knowledge as you can, because it will give you the comfort and confidence you need. I'm not saying it will completely solve all your hangups, but the knowledge and ability to make better decisions will ultimately lead to more success, more money, and more confidence in your numbers.

Nothing useful comes from being ignorant or uneducated about something. We've got to take responsibility for closing the financial literacy gap between men and women. We can't sit there and whinge about it; if we want to see change and we want it to be different, we've got to throw ourselves out there and do it ourselves. We've got to ask questions and fuck it up. We've got to put our big girl pants on and do it, even though we are shitting ourselves. It is the only way we're going to get change.

Think Like a CFO

Here is a super simple exercise you can use next time you experience negative beliefs or anxiety. When I have massive surges of anxiety, I use this exercise. It was taught to me by a psychologist when I was being treated for depression in my twenties, and it still helps.

1. Write a list of all the negative beliefs you have about the thing that's bothering you. It could be money, your ability to build your own business and wealth, or to go after a career you would love.
2. Alongside each, write at least two facts that disprove the negative thought.

Example:

Negative thought/belief: 'I'm useless with money.'

Facts to disprove this: 'When cash was tight last year, I stuck to a grocery budget and shopped in the discount sections to make it stretch as far as possible. I prioritised buying my kids new shoes and clothes over getting my hair and nails done.'

Use this regularly to prove to yourself that the negative beliefs you have about money could be all lies…

⚖️ If you have real deep-rooted anxieties around money, please speak to a professional. I can give you the tools you need to succeed, but none of that will matter if there are deeper problems you need to work on.

3

WHY YOU HAVE TO PICK A LANE

Why are you reading this book? Are you thinking about starting a business? Or do you just want to learn more about how money works?

Whatever your motivation, you need to know the deeper reason for it. If you are completely honest with yourself, you know why you are building that business. Or why you are curious about how money works. I don't buy it when people say they don't know; everyone has a reason for tackling money. And you need to know yours.

So, be honest with yourself: what is it? There are no wrong answers. But you do need to have one. If you want to build a business or you want to understand how money works, you have to know why.

Knowing *why* helps you understand *what* that money needs to do.

When you don't know what the money needs to do, you won't know how to get the biggest bang for your buck. You won't know where to put your focus, what your red flags will be, or how to invest your profits best. You will just be scrabbling around in the dark. If you struggle to remember why you started or are afraid to say the honest reason out loud, here are some reasons other people start their businesses or start learning about money:

- More time with the kids.
- Extra money and freedom to travel.
- Security.
- Control over your time.
- Freedom to leave home and start a new life.
- Buy a bigger house.
- Fund a personal hobby.
- Stick two fingers up to someone who pissed you off ten years ago.
- Fund a personal mission, a medical cause or a creative passion.
- Provide jobs for people in your community.
- You want people to think well of you.
- You want to have the financial power to buy whatever you want.
- You like the idea of leading people in business.
- You want to inspire people with your work.
- Leave a legacy.

So what's yours?

People want more money for endless reasons, and all of them are valid. Write down your reasons and be proud of them. There is no shame in wanting to make a ton of money or in never having to work a day in your life.

What Are You Building?

In this next section, I will share information that is important to anyone who wants to build a business, but even if that's not your goal, please keep reading. The lessons you will learn are as applicable to your personal life as they are to business.

In my experience, people tend to create one of three types of business, and each has a unique pathway to success.

They are:

1. A Lifestyle Business
2. A Legacy Business
3. A Business to Sell

What type of business do you plan on building? The type you're creating will determine which numbers you need to check and which operational aspects you should focus on. Someone who wants to build a business that runs without them needs a totally different set of guidelines and goals from someone who wants to grow their business to £1 billion a year revenue and five hundred employees. If you already have some experience in entrepreneurship, you may already know this, but it doesn't hurt to refresh your knowledge.

Everything you will read in this book has been tried and tested with companies I've worked with – or had sleepless nights over. I will explain how to recognise each type of business and then tell you about a real-life business and what we did together.

1. A Lifestyle Business

A Lifestyle Business is one built with the aim of funding the personal life you want, whatever that looks like for you. However, the structure of the business will vary massively depending on your individual priorities. For example, if you love travelling, it's expensive, so you'll need a lot more money than someone who just wants to make ends meet and be with their kids. If you want more flexibility because you're done schlepping into the city all the time, and you want to work from home, you will focus less on earning a shitload of money and more on building a business that gives you that flexibility. You might want to afford to buy expensive cars or watches, or you might have a hobby like running or art, or charity work that you want to pursue in your free time. A Lifestyle Business can be built around that, allowing you to tap into the community it creates and pursue your passion.

This type of business fits your lifestyle and gives you what you need, whether that's money, time or flexibility. However, there are some challenges.

People are quite naive about building this type of business and get frustrated when they don't see the flexibility and freedom they want straight away. Running a business, whatever your reason for doing it, is hard work, as it's usually all on you to generate that income. You have to dedicate a massive amount of time to getting the business started: getting new clients, networking, marketing and all that stuff. You have to make sacrifices now to make gains later.

It is also unlikely this type of business will generate massive amounts of profit because Lifestyle Business owners generally don't want to invest more than they need to into it. That means the business tends to reach a ceiling. That's not to say you can't generate lots of profit; you can, but it will be harder if your priority is time freedom and flexibility.

Case Study: School Run Studio

This online membership and subscription company was founded by James and Michelle, whose business goal was simply to earn enough money doing what they enjoyed and to live a comfortable life.

When I began working with them, they had been in business for four years and had published two books that had performed phenomenally well. However, the business barely met their financial goals: it was bleeding money and wasn't as tax efficient as it could be. Their business structure just needed tiny tweaks so they could get more out of their company. I had just left a corporate role and needed something lower pressure, so I put myself forward to work for them on a freelance basis. It was the first time I'd met anyone who wanted to build a business to create a lifestyle, rather than earn as much money as they could. It was inspiring. They were much happier to have the flexibility and autonomy of working for themselves than for someone else who could have paid them a lot more.

If you have a Lifestyle business or just want to know how to manage your personal finances better, this case study is relevant to you.

2. A Legacy Business

Legacy businesses are not necessarily focused on profit or revenue. Instead, they are often driven by a personal mission; also, they're usually quite big, with staff and expensive overheads to pay. It won't be just you and your friend working from your spare room (at least not for long). For example, I know someone who built her business based on helping women navigate endometriosis. That's quite a philanthropic motivator. But it was also partly driven by her anger at how poorly she was treated and how bad the system was when she was diagnosed. Another example is The Ova Co, started by two women who had fertility issues and wanted to create decent supplements for women going through IVF.

Building this type of business usually comes from wanting to do more with your life or wanting to make a change in the world. Companies that develop new drugs or new tech often fall into this category, as do ones which want to be perceived as the best in their industry, even if they don't make much profit or revenue doing it. On the flip side, the company's mission could be less altruistic than wanting to change the world: you could want to prove to your critics (or to yourself) that you can achieve success. Sticking two fingers up to your ex could also be a mission... and a perfectly reasonable one!

Case Study: Evergreen Assembly

This was a recruitment business founded by a guy with a very spiritual approach to life. Imagine a skinny, scruffy guy with dark hair and a massive beard. This founder decided he could do it better himself, and with two other ex-recruiters and me as their CFO, they created a Legacy-type business with the aim of turning over £200 million and having a headcount (employee count) of two hundred and fifty people. These business owners were aligned on their goal: they wanted to be the best recruitment business out there and to outperform their former workplaces. Within eighteen months, they'd grown from five to fifty people and were on track to reach their target.

However, as I mentioned earlier, this business had its dangers. By solely focusing on growth and headcount, they were running close to the wire in terms of profitability. They hired people based on reputation and made business decisions based on personal gain and emotion. Nonetheless, their revenue in such a short space of time was phenomenal and proved they were exceptional at building client relationships. Their ability to create a strong reputation despite their financial issues meant they achieved their business goals.

If you plan to run a Legacy business, you have to be honest with yourself. While it's fine to build one for personal reasons, those very reasons could detract from your success. You must ensure your personal mission doesn't prevent you from creating a sustainable and profitable business. Be honest with the people you hire, too. There's no shame in telling people your company was founded on a personal mission to prove to your shitty ex-boss they were wrong about you. There are plenty of people in the world who will work with you towards what you're trying to achieve — if you're honest about it. You can hire people who don't care about your mission at all and are happy just working for the money. But either way, be open about it. You don't want to end up with people who don't agree with your business goals: their dissatisfaction will be costly for your profits and your reputation. Make sure they understand your company's mission and are aligned with your cause.

3. A Business to Sell

The goal of this business is simple: financial gain.

Build something with enough value that it sells for a very high price, whether it's enough to pay off your mortgage or a massive amount for you to never work again. The type of businesses that fall into this category will vary, but the end goal is always to generate as much value as possible for the buyer, and they do that by solving a problem or building value. For some buyers, the value will be in its profitability or revenue. (Revenue is different from profit, and I'll explain all in Chapter 4.) For other buyers, the profitability or revenue won't matter. They will want to buy the brand name, the intellectual property, the client list, or the product line.

While this sounds like a lucrative business path, there are things to consider. Firstly, that final goal has to be the most important thing, so you'll need to plough everything back into the company: money, time and sleep. You have to be focused on giving up what you want now for what you want most later, and that will take a lot of dedication and discipline, especially on the days you don't feel motivated or do not see results.

Every decision you make will affect the value of your company, so you have to be razor-focused on your goal. There will be plenty of opportunities to react emotionally or be distracted by what your competitors are doing when sales are down. The sacrifices will be big, but if you build your business the right way, the financial reward will be worth it.

Case Study: Brass Tacks Collective

In 2013, I started working with a couple called Hannah and Simon, who owned a Tech analytics company. They started building in 2006, just working their connections and building things from scratch using their experience of working in IT at a large Tech firm, where they first met. They had a very, very clear goal: the whole focus of that business was profit and generating value, in order to sell. When I joined them, their business was mature enough that they had a finance team, but their processes were very inefficient; there was a lot of scrabbling around for paperwork and a lack of automation. And they had no cash whatsoever. (Yes, it is possible to have a business with no cash. I will explain this in Chapter 5.) When I joined them in September, their tax bill was due in December, and there wasn't enough cash available to pay it. They were not in a good financial position.

Within two years of me joining them, they sold the business and received $21 million: $15 million for the business plus $6 million in surplus cash.

If you want to build a business to sell, or are just curious about what's involved, this case study is relevant to you.

Now you know what types of businesses are out there, you can probably think of some examples:

- ✓ A Lifestyle Business: It's that Etsy store you love so much.
- ✓ A Legacy Business: The big London company your mate works for.
- ✓ A Business to Sell: Your old boss just sold theirs for a massive chunk of money.

Pick a Lane

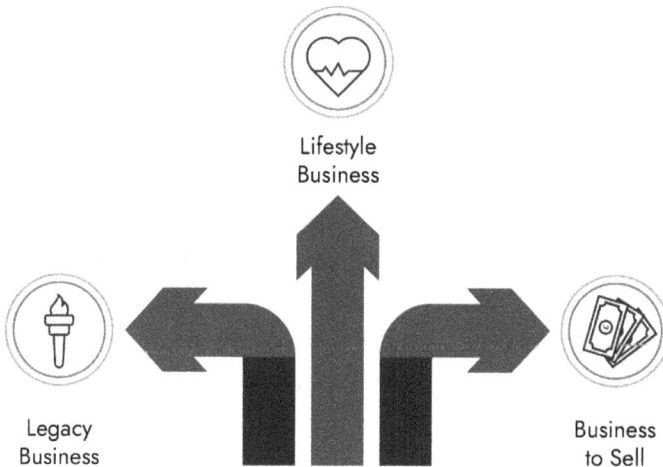

Lifestyle
Business

Legacy
Business

Business
to Sell

Money Matters

While businesses are all different, they have one thing in common: they all need to make money to survive. It doesn't matter if you're an ex-chemist and you want to create the next cure for cancer. Obviously, you're not on that mission to make a shit ton of money, but if your business doesn't make money, you can't fund that research.

Every business needs to make enough money to keep going. But *how* they do it will be different. In the next chapters, I'm going to show you how.

But first: a warning.

Don't Crash and Burn

Everyone has a ceiling within which they can work before they crumble, burn out or crash – even you. That means you need a clear indicator that tells you when the hard work is done; when enough is enough, and it's time to slow down or stop. Is it when you can comfortably pay your bills and have a little bit left over in case the boiler breaks? Or is it important to you that you drive a nice car, wear a nice watch and your kids go to good schools? Maybe it's a big number that you sell your business for or when your product is voted 'Best Product of the Year'.'

You need to know when you have done 'That Thing'; otherwise, how do you know when you've achieved your goal?

For simplicity, we'll call this indicator The Magic Number, but it doesn't have to be a financial goal. Your Magic Number can be the number of holidays you can comfortably go on, the number of free hours you have with your family per week or even the number of stories in the press about your company. It could be £15 million in profit, an employee headcount of two hundred, fifty extra hours with the kids, or three holidays a year.

Whatever your Magic Number is, it needs to be a clear and obvious sign to you that you have achieved your goal and you can stop and appreciate what you've achieved. Because what's the point of building a business if you can't stop and enjoy it?

So, stop now and write down your Magic Number. Don't play it safe; dream big and dream shamelessly. You don't have to tell anyone what your number is.

Write it here ➔ _____

Ok, great. Now, what's your real number? The more selfish one.

Write it here ➔ _____

No, the real one.

Write it here ➔ _____

Really? Try one more time.

Write it here ➔ _____

Ok - that's a good number.

Once you have that number, keep it somewhere safe. You will need it later.

Now you know what the three business types are and what your Magic Number is, we can move on to the sexy stuff: the numbers.

PART 2

KEEPING YOUR MONEY

KEEPING YOUR MONEY

·····································

It is human nature to make errors.
Especially with money.

How to Preserve, Protect and Promote Your Business

To help you manage your money and avoid costly mistakes, you will need to understand and make use of three key financial statements:

- A Profit and Loss Statement
- The Balance Sheet
- A Cash Flow Statement

These three reports help you measure your company's financial performance and financial stability. In other words, they work together to preserve, protect and promote your business:

- **A Profit and Loss Statement** → *Promote* → Reveals how well your business is performing and will help you grow.
- **The Balance Sheet** → *Preserve* → Helps you preserve the business by telling you how secure and financially stable you are.
- **A Cash Flow Statement** → *Protect* → Ensures you don't go bust by recording how much cash is literally 'flowing' in and out of your bank account.

(They are listed in this order because it's the order in which we present them as accountants. It is not indicative of importance.)

In Section 2, you will learn how these three mechanisms work together to give you an accurate picture of your business. This will not be as fun or sexy as learning about the best viral techniques to use on social media or which brand colours or fonts look the best on your website.

But it *will* give you the power to ask the right questions of your accountants.

It will empower you, and it will give you the knowledge to understand your finances and talk confidently about your numbers if anyone asks. After all, you don't have a business if you don't have money flowing through it.

If you choose one thing to remember from this book, to come back to again and again, come back to Section 2: How to Preserve, Protect and Promote Your Business.

MINI-CHAPTER:
NEED TO KNOW

WHEN THE NUMBERS BEND THE TRUTH

While numbers are black and white, accounting can be a little … grey.

The way in which we record our numbers can be nuanced and flexible. Just because a company records a profit or reports a sale, it doesn't always mean they've literally made a profit or had a sale – yet.

So, accounting is grey because there are two ways a business can do its accounting. Either with:

Cash-based Accounting.
or
Accruals-based Accounting.

Cash-based

When your business fits certain criteria (see https://www.gov.uk/simpler-income-tax-cash-basis/who-can-use-cash-basis for details), you're allowed to record your accounts on a 'cash basis'. This is when you only record the money as paid or received when it has physically landed in or has been taken out of your bank account. (It is worth noting here that some types of business are not allowed to use cash accounting, such as cemeteries, ministers of religion or waste disposal.)

Examples:

- As soon as the cash register opens, the money's gone in, or you swiped your card, that's when the money is made.
- If you're a service provider, you record the money once it's in your bank account rather than when you've invoiced a client.
- When you make a payment to a supplier or HMRC, it's exactly when the money leaves your bank.

There is absolutely no question about when that money has moved: it's time- and date-stamped. Whatever is left in your company's bank account is your 'bottom line' or Net Profit.

✎ Net Profit means your profits <u>after</u> tax and expenses have been taken. We will cover this in Chapter 4.

Accruals-based

If your business doesn't fit the criteria, you need to use accruals-based accounting. This is when you 'recognise' the money (record the planned transaction) in your books, but you might not yet have physically paid or received the money. So, you would record an invoice for money earned or a bill for a cost that you have incurred, but you haven't yet paid the bill or received the earnings. When you use accruals-based accounting, you can choose which date to record when the money was receivable or payable (in your Profit and Loss Statement) even if it hasn't physically gone into, or left, your bank account.

For example, when a builder gives you a quote for a house, they might charge you a deposit before they've done any work. That allows them to purchase materials and hire labourers. If an extension costs £100,000 and it's going to take six months, they could ask for £10,000 in month one, then invoice £50,000 in month four, followed by another £20,000 in month five, and the remainder upon finishing.

The builders could choose to record the money when they invoice you or when the work is complete, or they could split the earnings evenly across the time period, saying they made £16,667 per month for six months.

Revenue for £100k Extension						
Different Options:	Jan	Feb	Mar	Apr	May	Jun
Invoice Dates	10,000			50,000	20,000	20,000
Evenly Spread across project	16,667	16,667	16,667	16,667	16,667	16,667

It is the same with costs; you can choose to declare it on your Profit and Loss Statement when you get billed by your suppliers or contractors, or spread the costs equally across some months.

Unless you are a cash-based business, like a shop, cash-based accounting isn't particularly helpful as it doesn't really show you the business performance, but there are some tax benefits to using it: you don't have to pay your VAT bill until you've got the money in your bank account. It is beneficial in terms of managing your cash and not having to pay taxes earlier, and it's simpler. But that's the only real benefit. With accruals, you have to pay your VAT even if you haven't received the payments.

As you can see, accruals-based accounting gives you some leeway in the way you record your finances. You can choose the best way for your goals, as how you do it changes how your company appears to be performing. If you report that you sold nothing for two months, then sold £500k, then nothing, then £200k, that's very different to saying you sold £140,000 each of those five months.

£700k income across 5 months					
Different Options:	Month 1	Month 2	Month 3	Month 4	Month 5
Cash Based			500,000		200,000
Accruals Based	140,000	140,000	140,000	140,000	140,000

I will talk more about this in Chapter 6: Balance Sheets. However, this is where a lot of businesses get into hot water. While it is illegal to record incorrect numbers due to the way accruals accounting works, it is possible to draw attention to the positives and downplay the negatives (and vice versa). You should definitely ask your accountant about this, but accounting things like 'normalisation', 'depreciation' and 'amortisation' can significantly affect the way your business appears.

Okay, now you know about that, let's jump into Profit and Loss Accounts. Exciting stuff.

4

HOW TO READ THE MONEY DASHBOARD

— Profit and Loss —

In 2020, I worked for a company that supplied PPE during Covid. Obviously, during that period, they appeared to be doing really well and selling thousands of kits. You'd think they'd be making tons of money, right?

In reality, they were losing it. There was a hole in their numbers. They couldn't understand what was going wrong. They hadn't been tracking their numbers, so they had no way of telling where the problem was or how it had started.

Or how much money they were losing.

Soon after I'd joined them, I found the problem: they'd been over-charged £50,000 by a supplier, every month for eight months. That's a £400,000 hole in their business.

If the company had recorded their numbers correctly, they would have spotted the mistake much earlier. They would have realised that the numbers didn't add up, and they would have had an easier conversation with their supplier.

Why do I have to understand the P&L?

If you don't understand your P&L, you're running your business in the dark. It is like driving a car without a dashboard or running a social media account without checking your analytics. You have no idea if any of it is working. Without it you won't know:

- How much money you're making (or not making).
- How profitable your business is.
- How efficiently your business is running.
- How your past business decisions are affecting you today.
- How to look out for problems coming your way.
- How much corporation tax you'll have to pay.
- If you're spending too much or too little money.

A P&L tells you how well your business is performing financially. It helps you grow as it gives you clues about your profitability. Always get a professional accountant to help you create yours, but if you can't afford one yet, you can use online accounting software to create one. Otherwise, you can find some affordable freelancers on sites like Upwork and Fiverr. (Just be sure to do your due diligence first and make sure they're trained and experienced.)

🔨 Depending on the business, a P&L may also be referred to as:

- an income statement,
- a statement of operations,
- a statement of profits,
- an earnings statement,
- an operating statement,
- a profit and loss statement,

or some other combination of these words. Irritatingly, there is no standard name for it, and the title can vary across businesses, industries, and even within departments. In this book, I'll call it a P&L.

The P&L is usually reviewed on a monthly or quarterly basis, so you can track performance throughout the year. You compare it to your budget so you can make changes if you're falling short of your financial goals. (You will learn more about budgets in Chapter 7.) You can also (or instead) compare your current year's P&L to your previous year's P&L for the same period so you can measure the increase or decrease in your company's profit or its performance.

There is no single standard way to present a P&L internally, as variations will occur depending on the business. In this book, the P&L structure I talk about will focus on internal use, also referred to as Management Accounts or Management Information (MI). However, because filings with HMRC and Companies House demand a precise format, it's best to leave that to your accountant.

Next follows what an average HMRC formatted P&L looks like for a small business that does three to five million in sales per year. Compare it to the two examples of internal P&L formats that follow.

Average profit & loss		
Profit & Loss Account	This Year	Last Year
Turnover		
Sales	3,458,200	4,908,630
Interest Incomes	395	862
Gain on forex	8,950	7,620
Cost of Sales		
Purchases	-	-
Subcontractor costs	691,640	981,726
Hire of plant and machinery	-	-
Other Direct Costs	20,749	29,452
Gross Profit	**2,755,156**	**3,905,934**
Staff Costs		
Wages and Salaries	691,640	981,726
Directors Salaries	12,570	12,570
Pensions	40,000	40,000
Employer National Insurance	88,530	125,661
Temporary staff and recruitment	-	26,000
Travel	6,916	11,781
Motor	11,421	11,088
Other Staff Costs	2,981	3,670
Professional Costs		
Legal Fees	41,498	58,904
Accountancy Fees	22,041	31,247
Insurance Costs	17,291	24,543
Other Professional Fees	9,800	11,200

Average profit & loss (CONTINUED)		
Profit & Loss Account	This Year	Last Year
Business Premises Costs		
Rent	172,910	245,432
Rates	20,749	29,452
Lighting and Heating	1,245	1,767
Service Charges	4,150	5,890
Cleaning	1,556	2,209
Other premises costs	1,193	1,693
Use of Home	312	312
Other Expenses		
Telephone/internet	6,440	14,790
Stationery/printing/postage	350	21,850
Computer Software	5,570	14,580
Repairs and Maintenance	10,212	13,948
Bad debt	86,500	123,000
Loss on foreign exchange	4,475	3,810
Depreciation and Amortisation	144,710	45,480
Bank Charges	432	687
Interest Payable and similar expenses	-	-
Subscriptions	28,750	31,250
Travel and Subsistence	22,132	31,415
Other expenses	300	450
Corporation Tax Provision	246,711	367,111
Net Profit	1,051,769	1,603,419

Internal P&L Example 1		
Example 1	This Year	Last Year
Income	3,467,545	4,917,112
Cost of Sales	712,389	1,011,178
Gross Profit	**2,755,156**	**3,905,934**
Staff Costs		
Wages	704,210	994,296
Pensions and NI	128,530	165,661
Travel & Subsistence	40,470	54,284
Marketing Costs		
Advertising	57,500	62,500
Subscriptions	28,750	31,250
Entertainment	9,583	10,417
Overheads		
Property Costs	212,327	300,703
Professional Fees	90,630	151,895
Tech costs	12,010	29,370
Bad Debts	86,500	123,000
Depreciation	144,710	45,480
Print, Post & Stationery	350	21,850
Other	8,188	8,617
Corporation Tax Provision	233,966	362,256
Net Profit	**997,432**	**1,544,356**

Internal P&L Example 2		
Example 2	This Year	Last Year
Turnover		
Service 1	2,080,527	2,950,267
Service 2	1,387,018	1,966,845
Total Turnover	3,467,545	4,917,112
Cost of Sales		
Service 1	427,434	606,707
Service 2	284,956	404,471
Total Cost of Sales	712,389	1,011,178
Gross Profit		
Service 1	1,653,093	2,343,561
Service 2	1,102,062	1,562,374
Total Gross Profit	2,755,156	3,905,934
Expenses		
Staff Costs	873,209	1,214,241
Marketing	95,833	104,167
Office Costs	212,327	300,703
Professional Fees	90,630	151,895
Other overheads	251,758	228,317
Total Expenses	1,523,758	1,999,322
Corporation Tax Provision	233,966	362,256
Net Profit	997,432	1,544,356

Before You Read Your P&L

As I said earlier, this book does not teach you how to be an accountant, so I will not teach you how to put a P&L together. Your online accounting software or bookkeeper can help you with that. However, the one thing you need to be able to do is to *read* one when your accountant or your bookkeeping software gives you one.

At first glance, this can be overwhelming for anyone new to it. The first thing you need to understand is what each of those lines means. When you do, you're one step closer to financial empowerment. Even if all you do for today is learn how to read your P&L and spend the rest of the week recovering from the stress, take pride in knowing you took action. Take pride in that.

The following items or 'lines' have to be in every P&L. So get up close and friendly with these words:

Revenue (also known as 'Sales', 'The Topline', 'Turnover' or 'Income')

How much money do you earn (or would like to earn) from doing whatever it is you do? If you provide a service, how much money will you invoice the client for? If you sell a product, how much will you receive from the sale? That is your revenue, and it's always the top line in a P&L. Your revenue should be recognised (entered into your financial statements) when it is both earned and invoiced/invoiceable. The actual timing of the invoice and the money being received isn't relevant here. *Revenue is not the same as profit.*

Cost of sale (also known as Cost of Goods, Cost of Service)

How much does it cost to make your product? What is the price of the materials or ingredients? What are your subcontractor fees? This line is about costs directly related to performing the service or creating the product being made. You have some leeway with what you include here, but your expenses related to the creation of your product must always be recorded somewhere on the P&L.

When you have costs that are directly linked to the revenue you generate (like product costs or subcontractor expenses), it's important to recognise and record them at the same time as the corresponding revenue. So, if you enter revenue into your P&L in January and there are costs associated with it, they must also go into your P&L in January, regardless of when your supplier invoiced you or of when you paid the supplier. In accounting, this is called 'The Matching Principle'.

£700k income across 5 months						
Different Timing:	Month 1	Month 2	Month 3	Month 4	Month 5	Total
Invoices sent			500,000		200,000	700,000
Revenue Recognised	140,000	140,000	140,000	140,000	140,000	700,000

£420k cost of sales across 5 months						
Different Timing:	Month 1	Month 2	Month 3	Month 4	Month 5	Total
Bills Received	210,000	105,000		105,000		420,000
Matched Costs	84,000	84,000	84,000	84,000	84,000	420,000

Profit/loss across 5 months						
Different Timing:	Month 1	Month 2	Month 3	Month 4	Month 5	Total
Sent/Received Timing	-210,000	-105,000	500,000	-105,000	200,000	280,000
Revenue and Costs 'matched'	56,000	56,000	56,000	56,000	56,000	280,000

Gross Profit

If you want to know how efficient your core product(s) or service(s) are at turning the revenue they produce into profit, you look at Gross Profit. This is your revenue minus the cost of sales.

Gross Margin

This is Gross Profit divided by Revenue and shows what portion of your revenue you're keeping as Gross Profit.

Operating Costs (also known as 'Expenses' or 'Overheads')

Underneath Gross Profit are all your other day-to-day expenses involved with running your business. It could be employee costs: salaries, national insurance and employee benefits. You might have another line for office costs: rent, your service charges, cleaning and anything else related to your office. You could then have a marketing section where you would record any PR, branding spend or website updates.

I like to have sections for 'people', 'marketing', and 'operations'. It is completely up to you how you organise those sections, so go with whatever helps you track your business in the best way.

Operating Profit (also known as Profit Before Tax[17])

This is your Gross Profit (revenue – cost of sale) minus Operating Costs (expenses). Your operating profit is an indicator of the health and performance of your business.

Operating Profit Margin

Similar to Gross Margin, it's the operating profit divided by revenue. It shows what portion of your revenue you're keeping as operating profit. Basically, it is how much of the pie you have.

Tax

The tax you have to pay to HMRC is applied to your Operating Profit, plus or minus some adjustments. You may have to add back a few non tax-deductible expenses from your operating costs (e.g. depreciation, some client entertainment costs, some legal costs), but it's pretty much based on operating profit.

Interest

Any interest your business has earned on money in bank accounts, from stocks, shares or other investments. Also, any interest you've paid on loans or debts.

Net Profit (also called Profit After Tax)

This is what most people think of as their 'profit'. It is Operating Profit minus your corporation tax. Having a record of your net profit is essential because it demonstrates how much value you have created from your revenue for shareholders (or yourself if you are the sole director). Basically, it shows how efficiently you have converted revenue into profit after tax.

This profit figure is also the amount that's available to pay out to shareholders (or you as the sole director) as dividends.

EBITDA (Earnings Before Interest, Tax, Depreciation and Amortisation)

The simplest way to see this is: profit *before* interest, tax, depreciation and amortisation get deducted. So take your net profit and add *back* the tax, depreciation, amortisation and interest. It will be a bigger number than your net and operating profit, so it's a flattering view of your business performance.

This is a commonly used valuation metric when selling a business. You will hear conversations like, "This business is worth four times the EBITDA." It is a bit of a bullshit metric to be honest, but it gives a more flattering version of your profit.

Normalisation Adjustments

Sometimes you may have one-off costs during a year, such as restructuring costs or redundancies, which have nothing to do with the main operations of your business. Removing or stripping them out will leave you with a fair figure to compare against other years in order to measure your growth, without one-off costs skewing your numbers. This information will already be in the P&L, but we separate it out to show an 'adjusted' profit number.

It is also very helpful to restate your EBITDA to a 'normalised' value when you come to sell your business. You can strip out any costs the new owners wouldn't normally have to pay, so they can see what profit the business could make if they owned it. It is basically a more flattering version of your profit before tax that buyers use to decide how much the business is worth.

What Do I Do With All This Information?

Now that you know what each line represents, you have to find the total cost of each line. Yep, add up all those numbers.

Once you have that, work out what each line is as a percentage of your total revenue. To do that, you divide the total cost of each section by the total revenue. Like this:

Gross Profit Margin	
	This Year
Turnover	
Service 1	2,000,000
Service 2	1,500,000
Total Turnover	3,500,000
Cost of Sales	
Service 1	1,120,000
Service 2	705,000
Total Cost of Sales	1,825,000
Gross Profit	
Service 1 (2,000,000 - 1,120,000)	880,000
Service 2 (1,500,000 - 705,000)	795,000
Total Gross Profit	1,675,000
Gross Profit Margin = Gross Profit ÷ Turnover	
Service 1 (880,000 ÷ 2,000,000)	44%
Service 2 (795,000 ÷ 1,500,000)	53%
Overall Margin	48%

Then you use the percentages to gauge how well you're performing.

Looking at the image above, Service 2 makes less money (795,000 vs 880,000), but it is *more* profitable as it makes a 53% margin instead of 44%. This means you're making more profit on each sale of Service 2 compared to Service 1 because the costs are lower.

Most businesses have a standard percentage that is the norm. To find out what's normal for your industry, you can go to Companies House and find some P&Ls for businesses similar to yours. Or you can ask around and network with other business owners: what are they spending on materials? How much does it cost them to keep their staff? What percentage of revenue do they spend on marketing?

It is important you know what the normal spend is for your business type so you can understand if you're wildly overspending, being too careful or if the money is being spent in the right place. If you find out most chocolate brownie producers are spending, say, 60% of their revenue on their raw materials, that's a really good guideline for you. You can decide to spend more if you want better ingredients or less if it doesn't make much difference to your customers. When you know what the average ranges are, you can make changes within those guidelines with confidence that you aren't making bad decisions. But if you're wildly outside those ranges, something's not right.

Researching normal spend and comparing it to your own business is known as Benchmarking. It is important to help you make financial decisions, and we'll cover Benchmarking and KPIs in Chapter 9, so start researching now.

Say Hello to Your Shiny Crystal Ball

I often think of P&Ls as a business's crystal ball because they can tell you so much more about your business than you realise. Once you know what's normal for your business, it's time to start doing some readings.

→ When You're Spending Too Much

If you want premium chocolate in your brownies or you have been spending more on people because you want better staff, that's ok. However, if your P&L says you haven't had a good return in months – that is, your sales aren't going up or your operating costs are so high you're barely making a profit – you have a problem. You need to rethink your spending. It is clearly not working.

→ To Track Growth

If you're growing, your operating costs as a % of your revenue should go down over time as you become more efficient. A six-month period is the minimum timeframe you should use for tracking growth. If, after six months, it's increasing, you need to investigate.

→ To Find Out if You're Running at a Loss

Your net profit should not be a minus number. If you take your revenue, deduct all costs (operating costs and tax), and you are left with less than zero, you are making a loss. You have spent more than you are earning, and you need to fix that. The upside is you don't pay tax on a loss…

Comparative Profit & Loss		
Profit vs Loss Example	This Year (Profit)	Last Year (Loss)
Turnover		
Service 1	2,000,000	3,000,000
Service 2	1,500,000	1,750,000
Total Turnover	3,500,000	4,750,000
Cost of Sales		
Service 1	1,120,000	2,000,000
Service 2	705,000	1,500,000
Total Cost of Sales	1,825,000	3,500,000
Gross Profit		
Service 1	880,000	1,000,000
Service 2	795,000	250,000
Total Gross Profit	1,675,000	1,250,000
Expenses		
Staff Costs	873,209	1,214,241
Marketing	95,833	104,167
Office Costs	212,327	300,703
Professional Fees	90,630	151,895
Other overheads	251,758	228,317
Total Expenses	1,523,758	1,999,322
Corporation Tax Provision	28,736	-
Net Profit/Loss	122,506	-749,322

✎ Regardless of what type of business you're running, you should focus on two indicators:

1. Which line costs you the most. This is your 'biggest cost line' and one to keep an eye on.
2. Total spend as a percentage of your revenue. If the percentage is escalating, you have a problem coming.

So, now you know how to read a P&L. That is bloody brilliant and you're one step closer to achieving your Magic Number. In the next few sections, we'll look at P&Ls in practice. I will explain:

- The most important number on a P&L, depending on your business type.
- What guidelines you should use when looking at your P&L.
- And how, by looking at the P&Ls of School Run Studio, Evergreen Assembly and Brass Tacks Collective, I found ways to increase their profits.

Make sure you read all the case studies.

Remember:

1. **Be nosy.** Log in to Companies House and start looking at P&Ls from competitors and similar industries. What do you notice?
2. **Start recording your numbers today** in a way that is clear and helpful. Whether you have an accountant or are doing it yourself, go through your numbers and make sure they are recorded correctly.
3. **Be consistent in how you categorise your money.** As a business owner, if you're trying to track whether your business is growing, you need to set rules for recording your money at the beginning and stick to them. As you grow, you might realise that certain policies don't work anymore, in which case you can ask your accountant to redo the P&Ls under the new policies, but to have a decent and accurate picture, be consistent.

4. **Check your P&L regularly.** In general, your cost percentages should be going down. That means you're generating more money from your investments and costs, and you're starting to see a return. The flip side is that a downward trend is not always a good thing. It could mean you're underspending and delivering a poor service or product. If you've reduced the amount of chocolate in your brownies, for example, yes, you're going to see the cost go down as a percentage. But people might also start to think, "These are a bit crap," and stop buying them.

Think Like a CFO

How to analyse your own P&L (even if you don't have a formal one):

Step 1

- Identify the top three revenue sources of your business and the three most significant cost categories.
- Write down the risks your business faces for each of those three revenue and cost lines. E.g. losing a client, competitors taking more market share, bad economy, weather, international supply chains.

Step 2

- How will you manage those risks?
- To improve your business's profitability, can you increase your revenue or decrease your costs with any simple changes?

Step 3

- If you have a formal P&L, write down one red flag you've identified (this could be revenue or cost-related) that could be creating inefficiency or risk.
- Determine the root cause of the red flag, the potential long-term impact and one actionable step you can take to prevent/reduce the risk.

Profit and Loss in Practice: A Lifestyle Business

If you run this type of business, you probably don't give a shit about growth. Well, maybe you do, but it's not your goal. You are interested in making sure you have enough money in your pocket to live the life you want. Where you allocate your costs will be wildly different depending on the lifestyle you want and the business you have.

Here is what I mean:

- Want your business to run without you? You need to hire staff and invest in software to handle sales and transactions.
- Want to be able to buy yourself a new car every two years and go travelling around the world? Your personal costs will be a lot bigger.

Generally, the more money you need to fund your life, the bigger your profit number has to be and the more tax you will have to pay. You may be thinking, "Well, that's completely unachievable. My business is never going to earn that."

Let's not think small. Instead, think, *Okay, how can I make this work?*

In this case, look at your costs and strip some out. Work out your absolute non-negotiables: the things you cannot do without. What you can be flexible on? Can you hire an assistant rather than a manager? Can you do your own marketing until you can afford someone? Compromise and tweak what you can until you have something that is achievable and gives you what you want. You are building this business because you want a certain lifestyle, so make sure it does that or is at least working towards it.

The Most Important Number in the P&L

The most important number for you should be the Net Profit line or your Profit After Tax. If that gives you enough money to fund your life outside your business, it's doing well. So, what's that number? How much money do you need per year to fund your lifestyle? (This could be a good example of your Magic Number: the number that gives you the life you want.)

We are going to take that number and reverse engineer it. Get a pen and paper and play along at home with your own numbers. Let's see how much revenue you need to bring in so you can get the outcome you want.

Say you need £40,000 in your *personal* bank to achieve the lifestyle you want. (You can choose a bigger or smaller number or more for your own practice.)

$$£40,000 = \text{Lifestyle}$$

You have to pay around 32.5% of dividend tax on your income. To work out the amount you need *before* that 32.5% of tax is taken, divide that lifestyle number by 67.5% (67.5 = 100 - 32.5)

So:

$$£40,000 \div 67.5\% = £59,259 \text{ (Let's say £60k for simplicity.)}$$

$$\text{Your Lifestyle number} \div (100\% - \text{dividend tax \%})$$
$$= \text{Your Operational Profit}$$

40000/67.5% = just under £60,000. That is the *net profit* your company needs to make in order to pay that out to you in dividends.

$$£60,000 = \text{Your Net Profit}$$

Now work out how much *operational profit/profit before corporation tax* you need.

Corporation tax is roughly 25% in the UK, so we need to divide your net profit by 75% (75 = 100 - 25). It is the same maths as on the dividend tax we just worked out. So 100% - Corp tax of 25% = 75%. So, if your net profit is £60,000, you will need £80,000 *operational profit/ profit before tax* because:

$$£60,000 \div 75\% = £80,000$$

$$\text{Your Net Profit} \div (100\% - \text{corporation tax \%})$$
$$= \text{Your Operational Profit}$$

(We will cover tax in Chapter 10.)

Now, think about your business expenses. If your operating costs (rent, software, salaries, etc.) are £20,000, your business needs to make £100,000 in gross profit (i.e. profit from core sales). Because

$$£20,000 + £80,000 = £100,000$$

$$\text{Expenses} + \text{Operational Profit or Profit before taxes}$$
$$= \text{Gross Profit}$$

Finally, if your gross margin (the percentage you keep after paying for products or services you sell) is 40%, you need to bring in £250,000 in total sales revenue to get £100,000 in gross profit. (These aren't the exact numbers, but let's try to keep things simple.)

$$£100,000 \div 40\% = £250,000$$

$$\text{Gross Profit} \div \text{Gross Profit Margin}$$
$$= \text{Total Sales Revenue needed}$$

Congratulations! You've just reverse-engineered your business so you know how much sales revenue you need to give you the money you want personally.

⚖️ This is a very rough guideline to help you get started, and it doesn't take any notice of what level of personal tax you have to pay on other things. Be prepared for those additional costs.

School Run Studio

The first thing I asked James and Michelle was: How much do you need to have in your bank account every month to live the life you want? And then we worked backwards from that.

They weren't interested in making more money year after year or in investing; they just wanted enough to be happy. So, their costs were relatively small, and their most considerable expense was their marketing manager. For them, it was all about that bottom line, giving them what they needed.

Guidelines for Lifestyle P&Ls

- *Having a bit of slush is a good idea.* By slush, I mean a 10% contingency for the unexpected. If you have a month or a year where you've overperformed, you've got a little bit of slush there that covers the bad periods. Nothing ever goes perfectly. You will never hit £60k perfectly every year. One year you'll make £71k and £50k the next. So having a little bit of slush built in is a good idea.
- *Constantly monitor your costs* in case prices creep up. Costs will increase every year due to inflation. Your employees will expect a pay rise. The government might come along and whack an extra chunk of employers' national insurance on you. That subscription to your software might increase. Someone will go on maternity leave, so you'll need to pay for their cover. Stay on top of everything.

There will be constant tweaks and changes you must make to ensure you earn enough money to cover your costs.

So constantly check in: do you need to spend that money? Are you spending it in areas that benefit you and provide that lifestyle, or are you spending it for the sake of it? Be laser-focused on where every penny goes.

Profit and Loss in Practice: A Legacy Business

Every Legacy business will have a different metric for success, depending on the goal of that legacy. It is possible you won't be as interested in your P&L because profit isn't your main goal. You are more likely to focus on things not visible on your P&L, like how far away from going to market are we? Is the product performing well? Are people seeing success with it?

For many Legacy businesses, the profit number is just a mechanism for the goal, and their costs are just an investment in future revenue generation.

Here are some examples:

- If you're focused on developing a piece of technology, you will be in the development phase for a while. That means you will be losing money and spending more on operational costs.
- If you want to cure a terminal disease (I mean, fucking hats off if you manage that), that won't be a profitable business, either. Money will constantly be spent on investments in further research. You will be looking at who can help you fund this. What brilliant scientists have done this before? What else is in the market?

There is nothing wrong with spending more to achieve your goal, but you need to make sure you're not consistently losing money because, eventually, it's going to run out. No one wants to have to go to a bank, hands out like Oliver Twist and say, "Please sir, can I borrow some money?" They will look at your P&L and say, "You clearly don't know how to run a business," and slam the door in your face.

Remember: banks don't help you when you need it; they help you when you don't.

The Most Important Number in the P&L

The most important number for you should be your revenue.

If your costs are high because you're investing in people or operations, you must make sure you are still making money. You can't continually make losses and expect to carry on working towards that goal. A company has to make enough to be able to do another year or another month: you have to generate enough to stay in business. Otherwise, you'll have to close the doors and stop working towards that goal.

And that will be really frustrating.

Evergreen Assembly

For these founders, their goals were purely: 'How many people have we hired this year?' They didn't really care about their profit number; they just cared about hitting two hundred and fifty people and £200 million in revenue. You could say these were their Magic Numbers. Their staff cost line was increasing sharply, and their profit line was flatter because their costs were so high. But that was a risk they were willing to take. They were confident that the salespeople they'd hired would bring in the revenue – eventually. So, whilst I made recommendations on where to strip out costs to be more profitable, as the business owners, they chose how to spend their money. And they wanted to invest in growth by hiring more staff.

Guidelines for Legacy P&Ls

- *Track your biggest cost line year on year.* If your costs are increasing but your revenue and profits are not, you're spending money on the wrong thing, and it's not giving you a good enough return. Say, your cost line for ingredients is high because you've invested in luxurious chocolate for your brownies. But if people aren't buying them or aren't willing to pay more for them, you need to rethink that strategy.
- *Keep erratic spending to a minimum.* You may not mind if your numbers are crazy, flatlining for a couple of months and then going bonkers. You will be a lot less concerned about that because your goal is somewhere else. However, you can't achieve your goal without money, so always check in and make sure that spending isn't causing a loss.

You need to be very self-aware and to stay grounded if you're running a business like this. Hire an accountant or financial advisor who isn't afraid to tell you when you've gone too far. And *listen* to them. They are not someone to be frightened of; they are your sounding board and partner in finance. They don't need to be a full-time employee, either; you can hire someone on a freelance basis. You will learn more about building strong teams in Chapter 11.

Profit and Loss in Practice: A Business to Sell

If you want to sell your business eventually, its price will be based on its *perceived* value.

But there are loads of different ways something can be valued.

Imagine you're looking for a new laptop. You want to know how much memory it has, its weight and its battery life. Therefore, you do some research online, read reviews or walk into a store and ask questions to find one that fits all your needs.

For investors, it's the same. They will look for the value of the assets your business owns, its revenue, its profits, future revenue, or some other measurement the buyer thinks is important. And they will use your P&L to decide whether they want to buy and how much they're willing to pay.

Your P&L is your shop window.

It will show them if you're becoming more efficient year on year or less. It will show how much money you're making, if there's growth and if your business is worth buying.

🔨 Like a real shop window, you can dress up your P&L to make your business look more attractive or to attract certain buyers. But it must accurately and truthfully reflect what's inside the shop.

The Most Important Number in the P&L

EBITDA (Earnings Before Interest, Tax, Depreciation and Amortisation)

When valuing a business on the P&L, the value it's sold for is usually a multiple of the EBITDA number. If you want to sell for £12 million, and you know that businesses like yours tend to go for four times the profit, the EBITDA number needs to make £3 million per year.

£3 million x 4 = £12 million. (Obviously, there are other bits that go into it like tax, fees and so on, but this will be your ballpark figure.)

So, make your EBITDA number as big as you can, but don't be too cheap with your costs, either. You don't want to compromise the value your buyers get.

It is a fine balance to get right.

⚒ Want to work out how much money you'll get in your pocket after an exit? Use the Reverse Engineering Exercise from the Lifestyle Business section of this Chapter. Reverse engineering your EBITDA works the same way, but you go a step further to work out the exit value, and you swap out the tax percentages I used for the deductions you have to prepare for when you exit. You should definitely refer to someone like me or another corporate finance professional.

Brass Tacks Collective

Businesses like Simon and Hannah's generally sold for five times their profit, and they knew they wanted to walk away with $15 million. That meant we had to make their EBITDA number about $3 million. Remember: EBITDA is earnings *before* the deduction of interest, taxes, depreciation and amortisation (basically your taxable profit). So, we created a plan to get there, which I'll share more about later. The plan generated the profit they needed and helped them get to their goal far quicker.

But it wasn't just profit that helped them. They'd kept records of all their revenues and costs, reinvested almost everything they made back into the company and only took the smallest of directors' salaries.

If they hadn't been laser-focused on their Magic Number and used it to create a business plan, it probably would have taken them twice as long to get there.

Guidelines for Businesses to Sell P&Ls

- *Work with a professional.* If you're at the point of selling a business, you are probably working with an accountant who can present a 'normalised' P&L, which means stripping out costs from the statement that aren't relevant to the day-to-day running of the business.
- *Don't squeeze your costs just to make your profit higher.* If your costs are unusually low, buyers will look at the P&L and start asking questions. Low people costs could suggest your staff are underpaid or overworked. What does that mean for the new owners? Low-cost materials may suggest a problem with quality. Low operational costs: maybe your offices aren't well managed, or you're making shortcuts.
- *Show consistent growth in profit over the years it has been running, but not so much that it's capped out.* Your buyers will want to expand further. This means you must be very strategic about when you choose to sell. Get as much value from it as you can, but leave a little on the table for buyers, just not too much: otherwise, you'll regret doing it too early.

Your Magic Number, or your ideal sales price, is what you use to filter all your business decisions through. If you're at this stage of business, you probably have a CFO or financial advisor to manage these numbers, but as the business owner, it's important for you to understand how buyers will be looking at the P&L and, therefore, your business. You always need to keep an eye on that EBITDA number and ensure it's always climbing upwards.

5

EVERYTHING YOU KNOW ABOUT CASH IS WRONG (MOSTLY)

— Cashflow —

Whenever I meet a new client, the first topic of conversation is how much they worry about cash and how much it keeps them awake at night. It is the one thing that every business owner feels anxious about.

However, cash really is the simplest of all financial records and statements to manage. It is literally just the cash coming into your bank (cash inflows) and cash going out of your bank (cash outflows).

Yet business owners always get it so wrong.

How can a business owner who has made a massive profit then have no cash in the bank to pay their staff? Or you read the news that Big Bollocks Company Ltd is losing money despite receiving a million pounds of investment the year before. What's going on?

Making enough revenue or profit doesn't necessarily mean you have cash.

You're probably thinking, *Okay, I don't see how this is simple.* But the reason I say cash is the simplest is that, unlike a P&L, which is a little book of what's **about** to go out and what's **going** to come in, understanding your cash flow means being aware of the *actual* movement of cash in and out of your bank.

When you get your salary at the end of the month, it doesn't just sit there, does it? You have bills to pay (cash outflows), and the following month, you'll get your salary again (cash inflow). Sometimes, you have to find money for unexpected expenses, to replace a broken washing machine or plan that holiday you forgot you agreed to. So you always need cash sitting in the bank.

You have to do the same with your business. So, start thinking about your company cash in the same way you think about your personal cash:

- What do I have to pay?
- When do I have to pay it?
- And when am I going to get the money to pay for all of that?

The Cashflow Statement

Like a P&L, the cashflow statement is organised into several 'lines' recording the different cash inflows and outflows for your business. Your accountant will probably take charge of this, but it's good for you to know what you're looking at when it comes to analysing your own cash flow and making sure it's being managed efficiently.

Cashflow statements can look like this:

Cash Flow Statement (Direct Method)		
Cash Flow Statement as at 31st December 2025		
Cash Flow from Operating Activities:	Payments	Receipts
Receipt from Customers		1,500,000
Payment to Suppliers	600,000	
Overhead Expenses	100,000	
Wages & Salaries	250,000	
Income Taxes Paid	100,000	
Net Cash from Operating Activities:		450,000
Cash Flow from Investing Activities:	Payments	Receipts
Sales of Fixed Asset		500,000
Purchase of Fixed Asset	300,000	
Interest Received		100,000
Dividends Received		50,000
Net Cash from Investing Activities:		350,000
Cash Flow from Financing Activities:	Payments	Receipts
Equity Shares		400,000
Repayment of Loan	300,000	
Interest Paid	120,000	
Dividends Paid	80,000	
Net Cash from Financing Activities:		-100,000
Net Increase in Cash and Cash Equivalents		700,000
Opening Cash and Cash Equivalents		150,000
Closing Cash and Cash Equivalents		850,000

Cash Flow Statement (Indirect Method)	
Cash Flow Statement for the period to 31st December 2025	
Start of Period	31/12/2024
End of Period	31/12/2025
Cash Flows from Operations	
Net Profit	469,000
Add Back Non-Cash Expenses	
Amortisation	6,000
Depreciation	65,000
Subtract Gains, Add Losses	
Loss on Sales of Franchise Rights	8,000
Subtract Increases in Current Assets	
Increase in Account Receivable	-10,000
Add Back Decreases in Current Assets	
Decrease in Inventory	4,500
Decrease in Prepaid Insurance	2,000
Add Increases in Current Liabilities	
Increase in Account Payable	20,000
Increase in Income Tax Payable	4,000
Subtract Decreases in Current Liabilities	
Decrease in Wages Payable	-5,000
Decrease in Unearned Revenue	-6,000
Cash Flows from Operations	557,500

Cash Flow Statement (Indirect Method) (CONTINUED)	
Cash Flows from Investments	
Cash used to Purchase Equipments	-35,000
Cash From Sale of Land	80,000
Cash Flows from Investments :	45,000
Cash Flows from Financing	
Cash from Increase in LT Note Payable	15,000
Cash from Insurance of Common Stock	100,000
Cash from Paid in Capital	100,000
Cash to Pay Dividends	-190,000
Cash Flows from Financing :	25,000
Total Change in Cash	627,500

We should measure our cash in three 'buckets':

Cash from operating activities → cash generated by any business operation, such as money paid by clients or customers. It also includes recording money paid to suppliers.

> You will already have a record of these operating activities in your P&L, but the timing of paying them is important for cashflow.

Cash from investing activities → if you have bought or sold any business assets, they go in here. Similarly, if you have invested cash in company stocks or shares and earned interest or dividends, you record the cashflows here too.

📌 We also record asset purchases in the balance sheet when you get the invoice to pay for the asset, but the cash is marked as an outflow when you actually physically pay it. You see this in the 'asset' line in the balance sheet but with the timing of the cash inflows and outflows.

Cash from financing activities → any cash going in or out that relates to money borrowed or repayments of any debts. You also record any company stocks or shares issued where you have been paid in cash for them, or if you've paid any dividends out to the shareholders.

📌 The 'equity' line of the balance sheet is where shareholdings and retained earnings are recorded.

Your cashflow statement is a ***reality check*** on everything your business is doing, not just what it's generating from its operations. It shows how effectively the company is using its cash (the cash 'burn rate') and how 'liquid' it is.

How can a business be 'liquid'?

When you read the word 'liquid' or 'liquidity', what do you think? You might draw a blank, and that's ok. Maybe something to do with water...?

It is related to your cashflow. Like a flow of liquid...

Liquidity is the amount of cash and sellable assets you have that could pay off all your debts if you had to.

For example, if your bank were to come to you today, demanding you pay off your mortgage and your credit card bill fast, you'd check how much cash you had in your bank. What assets do you have that you could sell quickly? Your car? The house? Jewellery?

If you had enough cash or assets to convert into cash to cover those debts, we would say you were 'financially resilient'. In financial jargon terms, your business would have 'high liquidity'.

Low liquidity would mean the opposite, like owning a billion-dollar company, living in a mansion and wearing a designer wardrobe but paying for everything using credit cards and loans. You don't actually *have* any money that's yours. That is a pretty fucking *unliquid* situation to be in. So while your value could be in the multiples of billions, thanks to your business, your mansion, your car, your clothes and your stuff, if an investor or bank ever came to you to ask you to repay your debts, you would have trouble: it's not easy to sell a billion-dollar company or a mansion quickly.

Case Study: Lifestyle Business – School Run Studio

James and Michelle had made the classic assumption that the cash in the bank was a measure of how well their business was performing. They didn't have a ton of staff, and their revenue came in monthly, thanks to online subscriptions. Mentoring and 1-2-1 sessions were paid straight away, so they didn't really have any debts to chase. They had some expenses that went out monthly and some quarterly, and that was it.

Unfortunately, they forgot costs like their quarterly VAT returns or annual corporation tax. They overlooked the fact that if they paid themselves as directors and shareholders, they'd also have a personal tax bill, which they didn't bake into their monthly personal finances.

They had taken the approach of dealing with problems as they happen.

But that doesn't help you pay a £20k tax bill when you've been living month to month.

When you run a lifestyle business like this, plan for those regular monthly and annual costs. It's not about hoarding cash; it's about making sure you have enough and being disciplined with it. To solve James and Michelle's problems, we made sure everything was paid monthly and by direct debit, even switching the quarterly payments to monthly where possible. We opened an account with one of the newer online business banks and created 'pots' to set aside cash for future tax bills and the Christmas bonus they'd pay their marketing manager.

Due to the nature of their business, things often got quiet at Christmas as people decided to cancel their subscriptions to save money. Then, in January they would have an influx of people as the 'New Year, new me' mindset kicked in. So, they created a three-month cash reserve to help them manage the dry spells and topped it up when they had a more lucrative spell.

🔨 You only have to worry if your predicted three-month dry spell becomes a six-month dry spell: then you have to look at things a bit closer. Strip out non-essential costs, reduce your own costs and look for ways to reduce essential costs. Negotiate for longer payment terms with your suppliers and request early payment from clients. Have a big push on sales and sell off excess stock at a lower cost.

Cash flow for a lifestyle business is fairly simple: set up direct debits, set up extra pots or bank accounts for future costs, and be disciplined. If you do these things, your cash flow doesn't need to keep you awake at night.

Case Study: Legacy Business – Evergreen Assembly

These business owners were risk-takers. They made the bold assumption that they could make anything work: if they ran into a problem, they'd deal with it. Which, in some ways, I admire, because I worry about *everything*. As the CFO, I am usually the one staying awake at night worrying about it because it's my job to make it work. After all, my first responsibility is to make sure that a business stays in business.

This company's focus was on getting to £200 million in revenue and two hundred and fifty people, at any cost. But there were times when they had more money going out in bonus payments than they had in the bank. And then they wanted to hire another person. And take on a bigger office in Central London. The only thing that helped me to ground these founders in reality was some pretty pessimistic cashflow forecasts and drawing attention to how slowly their clients were paying. We changed all their processes to make cash inflows quicker, which soon helped improve their cashflow statements.

If you're running a Legacy business, you have to think of yourself as the warden of the company and of everyone who works there. Don't get so fixated on the goal that you forget you have hired all these people and given them jobs. They rely on those jobs to pay their mortgages and fund their lives. It borders on irresponsible behaviour if you run out of cash.

You *need* financial stability in order to achieve your goal.

Even though you are probably willing to take risks and to invest in things that might not work out (which in some ways is a wonderful thing; we need people who are willing to take risks), there's a balance between going after what you want and making sure you have a financially stable business to keep moving toward that goal.

Some wonderful things come out of these businesses, and they need to have that buzz and excitement. But ultimately, if the cash runs out, you're done. Therefore, focus on things like cashflow and make those little tweaks to improve your operations.

Case Study: Business to Sell – Brass Tacks Collective

When I first joined Hannah and Simon, they were doing the classic thing of flinging out an invoice and just waiting for it to get paid. They weren't paying suppliers early; they were actually paying things late, which is naughty. They weren't being proactive about getting the inflows, so they didn't have a healthy cashflow. They didn't want to chase their clients for payment. Instead, they were constantly looking at the bank account and asking, "What else can we sell?" to get that cash.

If you want to sell your business, you have to grow it large enough to become valuable enough to sell. And you need cash to fuel that growth.

We knew we had to get to a certain revenue number to make that sale price. The answer was simple: make little tweaks so they could invest more in the *growth* of the business.

If you want to improve your cash flow, do what I advised Brass Tacks to do: plan ahead for those bigger expenses that come once a year, prepare for the slower payments, and implement strategies that lead to faster cash inflows. Better disciplines and processes around invoices and more insight into where all the money is going on a monthly and annual basis will help.

Critical Cash

Now, let's stop for a second. Did you notice anything in the case studies mentioned? None of their cash issues came down to maths, but to operations.

Cashflow comes down to *timing*. All their cash flow problems came down to whether or not their payments were being made on time.

Do not underestimate how critical this is. It is far more efficient to find people who will pay you on time than to work for someone who pays whenever they like. When someone owes you money, and you have costs to pay, you have to find a way to pay it. That means:

- You risk putting in your personal cash to cover the shortfall.
- Taking out a credit card or loan with absolutely massive fees.
- Working with clients who aren't a good fit.

If you take the third action of working with clients you shouldn't take on:

- They negatively impact the perceived value of your business because you need the money fast. This could eventually affect the price you sell for.
- Or you'll have to work with an absolute nightmare client that you hate, that dents your self-worth and massively damages your brand.
- Or they don't pay at all; then you've worked for them for free.

What a fucking waste of time.

Cash is the fuel for your business growth, like the petrol in a car: you can't go anywhere if it runs out. So, if there's one thing you should pay attention to, it's your cashflow. Always prioritise having the most efficient cashflow possible. That means having faster inflows and planned, controlled outflows. When you have an efficient cashflow, you have choice and control over how you work and who you work with.

But you have to be disciplined.

How Can I Speed up Inflows?

For some businesses, like a lifestyle business, subscriptions and online payments are the most efficient. Money comes in as soon as it's billed; there's no delay or chasing. But when you run a business that relies on clients and companies paying invoices, things can get tricky.

Assume payments will be late → In the accounting world, we always practise prudence: we assume the worst. If your payment terms are thirty days, assume they'll pay in sixty days. If someone has a massive PO system that takes sixty days, assume you'll get paid in ninety. It's a massively negative way to look at things, but you should never run into cashflow problems, because you've planned ahead.

Encourage the behaviours you want → It is a good idea to encourage the behaviours you want from your clients as soon as you start working together, whether they're a small company or a big corporation. Demonstrate from the start that you expect your invoices to be paid on time. Pick up the phone and check they received the invoice, give them a chance to inform you of any upcoming problems, and administer a gentle reminder before it's due.

You could add a clause to your contract that says you'll charge interest if a payment is late, but what good is that to you? You don't really give a shit about the £2 a day you'll earn on interest. You need the money that they owe you. Do not be afraid to chase them.

Get into a routine of open communication → Develop a good relationship with clients, and they should naturally get better at paying you on time as they know what's expected of them. You can also use it to your advantage if you do run into cashflow problems, as you can ask for earlier payment, with a small discount if they agree.

How Do I Manage Outflows?

While you can't control when your client is going to pay you (unless you rock up to their doorstep with a bat), you can control when you pay your staff and your suppliers. I'm not for a second suggesting you should systematically pay them all late or pretend you have cashflow issues, because that's just crap.

But pay them when it's due. And not any earlier.

I understand why some business owners don't like the debt of supplier invoices hanging over their heads. It is uncomfortable to have what we perceive as debt. Yes, it is money that you owe, but it's money you're going to pay within the guidelines that person has set. Right?

If it gives you comfort to pay early, that's okay. But if you held on to it for an extra twenty days, you might earn a bit of interest on it before you pay, or have enough cash to pay that unexpected bill. If you have to pay early, wait until the day before, or get something for early payment: ask a supplier to offer you a discount. Yes, they'd be grateful for early payment, but you won't get a medal for it. It would be like choosing to pay for your groceries two weeks before you get them; nobody does that.

Hold off on spending your cash until absolutely necessary. By keeping it in the bank for a little longer, you can be more prepared for unexpected costs and maintain control over your cash – and your business.

If you run a business that has stock and you've purchased a year's worth of it, a lot of your cash will be tied up in that product. You won't have the ability to be fluid with your cash management. So, hold sufficient stock so you don't have delays supplying your customers because you have run out, but not so much that it hinders your ability to operate the business.

Use Your Cash Flow Forecast

If you're in the UK, you wouldn't assume the weather in the morning will remain the same that evening. You would give the weather report a glance in case you need to put on an extra layer or grab an umbrella. Right?

A cashflow forecast is the same thing.

You wouldn't open your bank account, see £200k sitting there, and think that means you're okay. Big mistake. You need to know how far that £200k will go.

Accountants use two types of forecast:

A twelve-month forecast → Use this to prepare for the year ahead and anticipate any massive problems that could come up. All it takes is for one invoice to be late or early, and your cash position has completely changed.

A thirteen-week forecast → Twelve weeks is enough to be quite accurate about how things are going to look, but the extra week gives you leeway to prepare for any problems that come up.

> Your accountant should be able to do this for you, but if you're just starting out, you can do this for yourself using reasonably priced accounting software.

Once you have your forecasts, you can map your costs and expected revenue across the year and prepare for them. But that all assumes that money arrives on time, which often it doesn't. So always practise prudence and assume that payments will be late.

What If It All Goes to Shit?

Say you lost your biggest client – your biggest source of revenue – what would you do?

You can't immediately stop paying your staff, can you? You would have to make redundancies; you'd have to give them notice. You would have to reduce some supplier costs, cancel some subscriptions and make other changes. You can't stop your outflows overnight.

This is why I always bang on to my clients about this: have three months of cash in reserve.

It is probably quite obvious why we all should do this, yet you'd be surprised how many business owners don't keep cash in reserve. My clients ask, "Well, how much difference could it make in three months? Why do I need that much?" If you have three months of cash in reserve, you almost end up buying yourself six months because of the lower costs, and extra time to pick things back up.

No bank lender will give you cash if you, as a business, run out. It's too risky. They will only give it to you when you are doing well. So you've got to solve it yourself. You need to see those things coming. This is why we do the long forecast and the short one, and keep it up to date.

Whether you are building a legacy business, a lifestyle business, or are building up to sell, everyone should have three months of coverage. I realise that's not always possible when you're in startup mode, but if you want to take away the worry about running out of cash, having that three-month reserve will buy you enough time to sort out any problems that come in.

The Cash Flow Essentials

If you're at that size where you can afford to work with an accountant, do it, and they can take that burden off you. However, whether your business is doing really well or really badly, you always need to stay close to your cash.

1. Open Pots

If you have an accountant or CFO, they will manage this all for you (if you ask them to). But if you're not there yet, set aside 'pots' or open extra bank accounts to save up for future tax bills, future bonuses, VAT and any other quarterly or annual costs you're likely to forget about. As a company, you can have as many as you like. Create a VAT one, a corporation tax one, or whatever else you need. Do this for your self-assessment, too.

2. Improve Your Inflows and Outflows

Control when you pay people and negotiate better terms for money coming in. Increase the speed of your inflows and slow down the outflows. Create open communication with suppliers and clients and develop positive relationships that will help you in times of need.

3. Keep Cash in Reserve

Work out how much money you'd need in reserve if you experienced three months without any income. If your P&L shows that you spend £10,000 a month, make sure your cash balance doesn't fall below £30,000. In an ideal world, you'd have more, but three months is the minimum. And, coincidentally, it ties neatly together with your thirteen-week forecast.

4. Use Your Cashflow Forecasts

Even if your accountant manages this, be aware of how and when your cash flows in and out of our business. Plan everything, because it will go wrong at some point.

5. Be Obsessive

Know everything about your cashflow to the point of obsession. Know enough about it that you could almost predict a problem before it arises. Do not wait for the problem to find you.

Think Like a CFO

1. Make a list of all your business's cash inflows (how money comes in) and cash outflows (how money goes out).
2. Make a list alongside any of these which could become cash 'blockers'. For example, an inflow block would be slow-paying clients. An outflow block would be things you can't pay late without impacting your business, e.g. stock suppliers. Things that are most likely to cause problems, basically.
3. Write one step you could take to solve or reduce any blockers you identify.

MINI-CHAPTER: NEED TO KNOW

DOUBLE ENTRY

(YES, I FIND THIS PHRASE AMUSING)

Any transaction that happens in a business hits two places, whether that's a sale, a cost or paying your staff: any kind of thing that goes in your accounts. That's why we call it 'double entry'. (I do enjoy saying this phrase because it makes me laugh, but that's because I'm an absolute child.)

When you send an invoice to your client, it hits two places:

1. Your **balance sheet** as money that someone owes you.
2. Your **P&L** as revenue that you have generated.

When that invoice gets paid:

1. It clears the **balance sheet** because the debt has been wiped off.
2. It gets logged in your **cash** as inflow.

Here are some more examples:

Example 1

When we buy a computer, we log it as:

> (1) an *asset* and

> (2) a *cash outflow.*

When we depreciate that asset, we:

> (1) reduce the **Balance Sheet** value and

> (2) charge that to the **P&L** as a cost we have incurred.

If we sell that asset, we:

> (1) remove it from the **Balance Sheet** and

> (2) charge any upside/downside to the **P&L**.

✎ To depreciate an asset means to spread out the cost of an asset over time. When you purchase an asset, such as a laptop, its value drops over time due to wear and tear; it decreases in worth. Instead of recording this asset purchase as a one-off cost, you spread the cost over its useful life.

Example 2

When a supplier invoices us, we log it as:

> (1) a *debt* on the **Balance Sheet**, and

> (2) a *cost* on the **P&L**.

When we pay that supplier, we:

> (1) remove the debt from the **Balance Sheet** and

> (2) log it as a cash outflow.

It is an accountant's checking mechanism. It's how we know we have recorded everything, because it has to hit two places, and it has to match. We haven't missed anything, and we can be confident that this is an accurate portrayal of this company.

It is called a balance sheet because if you've done everything right, the top half matches the bottom half: it's balanced. If your balance sheet doesn't balance, you've cocked something up.

If you want to learn more, check out the Balance Sheet video on my YouTube Channel @FeistyFD.

6

YOUR BUSINESS'S REPORT CARD

— Balance Sheets —

Imagine you have a conversation with a potential investor. They look at your balance sheet and frown. They say, "Your revenue looks good, but your balance sheet shows a high level of short-term liabilities compared to assets. How do you plan to address this if a client payment is delayed?"

For most people new to financial literacy, this might sound like another language. Your brain might have just switched off. But if you look past the jargon, the investor is really asking, "You have more outgoings and debt than things of value. What happens if a payment to your business is delayed? Will your company survive?" (Yeah, I don't know why they don't just say that, either. But that's finance.)

Another question you might get is, "You've made decent profits the past few years; why are your cash reserves so low?" In reality, they want to know, "Have you just paid out all the profits to yourself in dividends instead of reinvesting in growth?"

This is how knowing your balance sheet will give you proof and the unshakeable confidence to say, "I know how to make good business decisions. My business is thriving and here's why." It is a neatly packaged statement that tells anyone who's interested how well-managed your company has been and what it's worth to the shareholders. It tells people if your company can ride out upcoming market storms, if your company is worth investing in, and how well you manage your cash.

In summary, it tells people how strong or weak your company is. In my opinion, it's the Holy Grail.

Unfortunately, it's the document that's the most ignored. I don't know why. As an accountant, it's my favourite place to be. (Sorry, that's really nerdy, isn't it?) It tells you everything, a bit like a report card:

- All profits and losses ever made that haven't been paid out in dividends.
- What money is owed and what is owed to you.
- How much cash you have.
- How liquid the company is.
- What you've bought.
- What you've sold.
- What you own.

Like I said, the Holy Grail.

We All Have a Balance Sheet

Every person you know has skills, knowledge and experience to share with others that create value. Maybe it's easy for you to make people laugh, or you're a great artist. Maybe you are the only person in your friendship group who actually *likes* eating salad. But we all have bad habits or negative traits, too. An addiction to junk food or smoking. Perhaps a lack of skills in a certain area, or maybe we overthink and procrastinate. Some people may have trouble keeping their emotions in check or turn to self-destructive behaviours when stressed.

If someone has been working on the positives in their life (gaining new skills, making friends, exercising), you could say they have more 'assets' and are more likely to have longevity and get more out of life. If their bad habits are out of control, such as excessive drinking, an anger problem, or no exercise, you could say there will likely be problems ahead. They have 'liabilities'.

We do the same in business. We subtract the negatives from the positives to assess a business's financial health. This overview is important for understanding a company's long-term stability. Here is what an average Balance Sheet looks like.

Balance Sheet Example	
Balance Sheet as at 31 December 2025	
Fixed Assets	
Land and Buildings	10,000
Motor Vehicles	20,000
Computers	30,000
Furniture	40,000
Machinery	50,000
Total Fixed Assets	150,000
Depreciation	
Land and Buildings	6,000
Motor Vehicles	7,000
Computers	8,000
Furniture	9,000
Machinery	10,000
Total Depreciation	40,000
Value of Fixed Assets	110,000
Current assets	
Bank Account - Current	200,000
Bank Account - Savings	100,000
Cash	300,000
Prepayments	20,000
Accounts Receivable	250,000
Total Current Assets	870,000

Balance Sheet Example (CONTINUED)	
Less Current Liabilities	
Accounts Payable	80,000
Loan	150,000
Accruals	210,000
Total Current Liabilities	440,000
Net Assets	540,000
Equity	
Opening Balance	40,900
Shareholder funds	100
Retained Earnings	499,000
Total Equity	540,000

The main categories are:

Assets – what you own
Liabilities – what you owe
Equity – shareholder value

Let's look at what each of these means in detail.

1. Assets

What brings value? What do you have that keeps your business going?

- **What your business owns:** offices, buildings, computers and furniture (not what we paid for them because we've depreciated them), stock or inventory and cash.
- **Accounts receivable:** invoices you've sent to clients that have not yet been paid.
- **Prepaid costs/expenses** such as quarterly rent paid in advance. This is an asset because it represents that you'll get something in return for the cash you've paid.

2. Liabilities

What could cause problems? What obstacles or challenges do you have to prepare for?

- **Debts:** money you owe to others, such as supplier invoices not yet paid in cash, loans not yet repaid, and any money owed to HMRC, like corporate tax, VAT and payroll taxes.
- **Costs due to be paid** such as annual bonuses or company events.
- **Money paid in advance:** payments you have received from clients in advance of work being done.

3. Equity

(Also called shareholders' equity, stockholders' equity, or net worth)

- Your overall value once you deduct liabilities from assets.

✎ Equity is the value of what you own. It is the amount of money you'd get after an asset is sold and any debts are paid off. If you own a million-pound house and you have an £800k mortgage, your equity is £200k. It is the difference.

- **Company value:** what the company is worth, specifically to shareholders.
- **Share capital:** the value of shares held in the company.
- **Reserves:** the cumulative profits of the company minus any dividends declared.

Assets, liabilities and equity are displayed in different sections on your balance sheet, and they have to 'balance', hence the name. It can be shown in slightly different ways, but ultimately a balance sheet shows:

Assets = Liabilities + Equity
OR
Equity = Assets - Liabilities

Be an Asset, Not a Liability

When analysing your balance sheet, you'll want to compare snapshots either year by year or quarter by quarter. You can do month by month if you want. Whatever business you run, you always want to have a positive and strong balance sheet. This means you have *more assets* than liabilities and, therefore, more value, especially for any shareholders or owners. It is a business that is more likely to survive setbacks and problems. If you ever want to attract investors or need a business loan from the bank, you'll want to present a business worth investing in: one with a healthy balance sheet. Even if your accountant is the one plugging in the numbers, when you ask to see your balance sheet, this is what to look for:

How to Avoid a Weak or Negative Balance Sheet

→ *Make sure your liabilities are not bigger than your assets*. If they are, you have a problem. It means you have more debts or money owed elsewhere than you have to come in, and that puts your business in a fragile position.

Negative Balance Sheet Example	
Negative Balance Sheet	
Fixed Assets	
Land and Buildings	10,000
Motor Vehicles	20,000
Computers	30,000
Furniture	40,000
Machinery	50,000
Total Fixed Assets	**150,000**
Depreciation	
Land and Buildings	6,000
Motor Vehicles	7,000
Computers	8,000
Furniture	9,000
Machinery	10,000
Total Depreciation	**40,000**
Value of Fixed Assets	**110,000**
Current assets	
Bank Account - Current	200,000
Bank Account - Savings	100,000
Cash	100,000
Prepayments	20,000
Accounts Receivable	200,000
Total Current Assets	**620,000**

Negative Balance Sheet Example (CONTINUED)	
Less Current Liabilities	
Accounts Payable	380,000
Loan	195,000
Accruals	210,000
Total Current Liabilities	785,000
Net Assets	- 55,000
Equity	
Opening Balance	40,900
Shareholder funds	100
Retained Earnings	- 96,000
Total Equity	- 55,000

→ *Don't keep adding liabilities to the sheet;* that would indicate that you've borrowed money, not managed to pay it back very well and had to borrow more from someone else. Who do you owe money to? Is it HMRC or is it a loan from a bank? If it's HMRC, that's a reasonable debt, but if you have several debts to banks or individuals that haven't been used to invest in growth, then there's a problem.

Do not get into a position where you try to ride out debt by continuing to borrow more money. At some point, the loans will stop. If you can't pay off your debts, you'll have to go insolvent. That means your company is unable to pay its debts, and the people you owe money to will take action to recover those loans. That is a red cross against your name, and you'll almost certainly have to close the business down.

High Debt Balance Sheet Example	
High Debt Balance Sheet	
Fixed Assets	
Land and Buildings	10,000
Motor Vehicles	20,000
Computers	30,000
Furniture	40,000
Machinery	50,000
Total Fixed Assets	**150,000**
Depreciation	
Land and Buildings	6,000
Motor Vehicles	7,000
Computers	8,000
Furniture	9,000
Machinery	10,000
Total Depreciation	**40,000**
Value of Fixed Assets	**110,000**

High Debt Balance Sheet Example (CONTINUED)	
Current assets	
Bank Account - Current	50,000
Bank Account - Savings	50,000
Cash	50,000
Prepayments	200
Accounts Receivable	80,000
Total Current Assets	**230,200**
Loan outweighs current assets	
Less Current Liabilities	
Accounts Payable	380,000
Loan	250,000
Accruals	210,000
Total Current Liabilities	**840,000**
Net Assets	**- 499,800**
Equity	
Opening Balance	40,900
Shareholder funds	100
Retained Earnings	- 540,800
Total Equity	**- 499,800**

→ *If your assets are getting bigger* and bigger over time, it means you're making a lot of purchases. That is not a bad thing, but it depends on what you're buying and what the reason is. Is it buildings or is it laptops? Is your accountant depreciating them on the P&L and at the right rate?

Comparative Balance Sheets (Assets Increasing)			
Balance Sheet as at 31 December 2024		Balance Sheet as at 31 December 2025	
Fixed Assets		Fixed Assets	
Land and Buildings	10,000	Land and Buildings	10,000
Motor Vehicles	20,000	Motor Vehicles	20,000
Computers	30,000	Computers	40,000
Furniture	40,000	Furniture	40,000
Machinery	50,000	Machinery	80,000
Total Fixed Assets	150,000	Total Fixed Assets	190,000
Depreciation		Depreciation	
Land and Buildings	6,000	Land and Buildings	8,000
Motor Vehicles	7,000	Motor Vehicles	9,000
Computers	8,000	Computers	10,000
Furniture	9,000	Furniture	11,000
Machinery	10,000	Machinery	20,000
Total Depreciation	40,000	Total Depreciation	58,000
Value of Fixed Assets	110,000	Value of Fixed Assets	132,000
Current assets		Current assets	
Bank Account - Current	200,000	Bank Account - Current	100,000
Bank Account - Savings	100,000	Bank Account - Savings	100,000
Stock/Inventory	300,000	Stock/Inventory	200,000
Prepayments	20,000	Prepayments	30,000
Accounts Receivable	250,000	Accounts Receivable	260,000
Total Current Assets	870,000	Total Current Assets	690,000

Comparative Balance Sheets (Assets Increasing) (CONTINUED)			
Balance Sheet as at 31 December 2024		Balance Sheet as at 31 December 2025	
Less Current Liabilities		Less Current Liabilities	
Accounts Payable	80,000	Accounts Payable	80,000
Loan	150,000	Loan	200,000
Accruals	210,000	Accruals	180,000
Total Current Liabilities	440,000	Total Current Liabilities	460,000
Net Assets	540,000	Net Assets	362,000
Equity		Equity	
Opening Balance	40,900	Opening Balance	40,900
Shareholder funds	100	Shareholder funds	100
Retained Earnings	499,000	Retained Earnings	321,000
Total Equity	540,000	Total Equity	362,000

Or are you buying stock? That would raise questions about how well you're managing your stock and inventory. If that stock is perishable, is it a good idea to hold too much of it? Holding too much stock suggests you might have problems with stock management and inventory. Holding too much stock also ties up too much cash and is a sign of poor operational processes.

High Stock Balance Sheet Comparison

Balance Sheet as at 31 December 2024		Balance Sheet as at 31 December 2025	
Fixed Assets		Fixed Assets	
Land and Buildings	10,000	Land and Buildings	10,000
Motor Vehicles	20,000	Motor Vehicles	20,000
Computers	30,000	Computers	30,000
Furniture	40,000	Furniture	40,000
Machinery	50,000	Machinery	50,000
Total Fixed Assets	150,000	Total Fixed Assets	150,000
Depreciation		Depreciation	
Land and Buildings	6,000	Land and Buildings	8,000
Motor Vehicles	7,000	Motor Vehicles	9,000
Computers	8,000	Computers	10,000
Furniture	9,000	Furniture	11,000
Machinery	10,000	Machinery	20,000
Total Depreciation	40,000	Total Depreciation	58,000
Value of Fixed Assets	110,000	Value of Fixed Assets	92,000
Current assets		Current assets	
Bank Account - Current	200,000	Bank Account - Current	100,000
Bank Account - Savings	100,000	Bank Account - Savings	100,000
Stock/Inventory	200,000	Stock/Inventory	300,000
Prepayments	20,000	Prepayments	30,000
Accounts Receivable	250,000	Accounts Receivable	240,000
Total Current Assets	770,000	Total Current Assets	770,000

High Stock Balance Sheet Comparison (CONTINUED)			
Balance Sheet as at 31 December 2024		Balance Sheet as at 31 December 2025	
Less Current Liabilities		Less Current Liabilities	
Accounts Payable	80,000	Accounts Payable	80,000
Loan	150,000	Loan	150,000
Accruals	110,000	Accruals	240,000
Total Current Liabilities	340,000	Total Current Liabilities	470,000
Net Assets	540,000	Net Assets	392,000
Equity		Equity	
Opening Balance	40,900	Opening Balance	40,900
Shareholder funds	100	Shareholder funds	100
Retained Earnings	499,000	Retained Earnings	351,000
Total Equity	540,000	Total Equity	392,000

→ *Watch your debtors' line.* If your debtors' line (the people who owe you money, like clients) is going up month on month, that means you're not getting paid. That's an operational issue and a major problem for any business.

→ *If your cumulative profit (reserves) line is not increasing,* there's an issue. Your cumulative profit is all the profits you've ever made and have left in the business. So if your cumulative profit line is not increasing, despite you managing your cash effectively, your debtors' line being fine, and you haven't got a load of borrowings, it might mean that the shareholders are simply taking all the money out. If it's your company, and that's your intention, that's fine. However, there's a fine line between withdrawing enough for the business to be viable and rewarding for you as a shareholder and the level of withdrawals being harmful to the business.

How to Ensure a Strong or Positive Balance Sheet

→ *A wavy debtors' line.* If you were to track your debtors on a graph (how much money your clients owe you), that line should go up and down in a little wave; it's a good sign as it means invoices are going out, and they're getting paid. If it's going up and your cash is going down, you've got a problem with cash collection.

Debtors Increasing

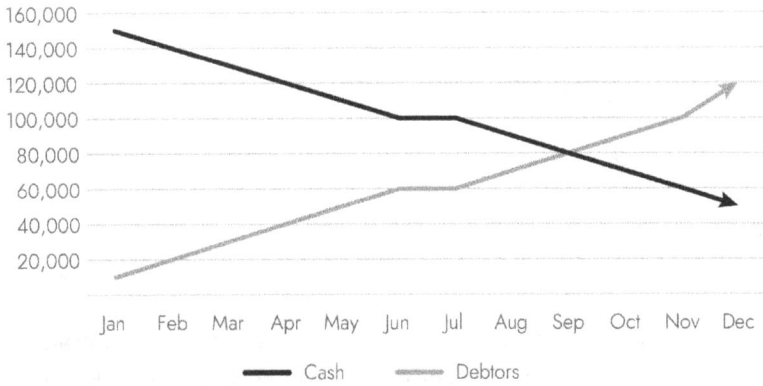

Debtors and Cash Flowing Correctly

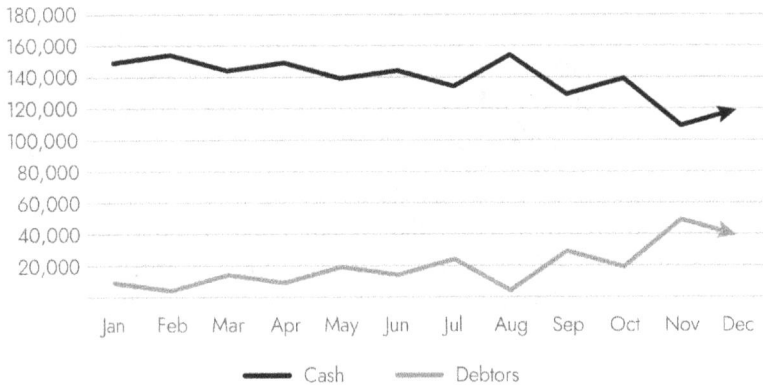

→ *Your assets should be worth more than your liabilities.* You want to see that number getting bigger over time because it means that your company's growing. It means you're making profits, reinvesting them in the right way and managing your cash well. You are not paying out too much of your profit in dividends to the shareholders, either. A business that's progressively getting more positive is a sign of a strong business. You want to see a healthy growth curve with the debts going down and the cash going up.

🔨 Balance sheets will vary by business type and industry. Service businesses won't have a line for inventory because they don't have stock and hold fewer assets. Other companies may own bigger assets, such as office buildings or computers.

Case Study: Lifestyle Business – School Run Studio

Even though I think the balance sheet is the holy grail of accounting, it's not that important for people who run lifestyle businesses. You won't care about building shareholder value because you're taking it all out to spend on yourself. For James and Michelle, the financial stability of their business was measured month to month, and it went up and down throughout the year.

As long as it was stable enough to fund the next month, that was all that mattered to them. They had no products and no stock; they owned a couple of laptops, had a few hundred pounds in cash and had one employee. Their balance sheet was minuscule because they weren't running it for growth; they were running it to fund the lifestyle that they wanted.

If you're running a Lifestyle business, all you need to do is keep your balance sheet out of the negative. Keep it positive with a little bit of slush for some difficult periods. Everyone runs into trouble sometimes, so as long as you have another plan for what you would do if things started to go wrong, you'll be ok. James and Michelle could never have gone to a bank and borrowed money because the bank would have just laughed at them; they didn't have any assets that a bank could secure a loan against. But they had friends and family they could rely on. If you're not in a position to have a personal backup, make sure that there is enough stability shown on your balance sheet that if you had to go and get borrowings, you could.

Running a business to give you just enough money to get by is high risk, especially if you have no backup or assets you could sell to cover debts or long-term investments. On the flip side, if you're running a lifestyle business with the goal of owning a shitload of cars or houses, you're not going to have a resilient company. But you are more likely to have plenty of personal assets you could fall back on if you needed the cash.

As long as you have three months of funds, as I mentioned in Chapter 5, that's your backup. Apart from that, you're relying on clients or customers. Make sure you find other ways to support your business in case anything goes wrong.

Case Study: Legacy Business – Evergreen Assembly

Legacy businesses tend to be high risk because they are about building for a reason other than profit. Therefore, your balance sheet may either be positive or negative depending on the company's goals and long-term spending.

Evergreen Assembly was a service business, so their balance sheet was fairly small. Their assets were small; all they had were laptops, computers and furniture, the money owed to them by clients and their cash.

But their liabilities were huge: they loaned cash to staff and hired people too quickly. They didn't wait for their staff to make sales before taking on another batch. The owners paid themselves huge salaries, even though they owed a million dollars in startup costs to their founder's family. Even their £20 million in annual revenue couldn't cover these costs.

Their balance sheet was massively in the red, and they were making no profit. Their solution (not one I recommend at all!) was to get a few clients to agree to pay a few million in advance for three years of work. But that's an advance for work not yet done. By being bullish about their ability to use that cash to grow, they would soon end up back in the red.

If you're running a Legacy business, it's okay to have a negative balance sheet (meaning the final number at the bottom is negative) if your growth plan is *sustainable and reasonable.*

If you've borrowed a million dollars because you need to invest in new research, of course, you'll be in a poor position for a couple of years. Lots of tech firms have awful balance sheets because they're in the startup phase or in research and development. Until they actually go to market and start selling a product, it will look horrible on the balance sheet. But you must *always* be growing in a way that is sustainable and secure. If everyone you owe (your creditors) come knocking on the door and want their money back, you need to be able to pay it. Also, you need to have enough cash to fund your entire business for three months, should anything bad happen.

As well as the three months of coverage, a legacy business may need an additional money pot to fund the next round of research or the planned level of growth. As long as you've put that security in place, great. What an incredible thing to do to build a legacy.

Case Study: Business to Sell – Brass Tacks Collective

When I joined Brass Tacks Collective, their balance sheet told me their company wasn't resilient. It was a positive balance sheet, but they didn't have enough cash to grow their company.

The goal was to sell this business, and a large part of the deal was based on the balance sheet. We structured the deal so the company was bought on a cash-free, debt-free basis. That means the buyer is left with enough cash to fund the business for three to six months, and the sellers get to keep any surplus cash that's left after clearing all the debts.

As I had forced Hannah and Simon to be frugal and so cautious with how they grew the business, they were able to walk away with about $6 million in surplus cash, *in addition* to what they made from the EBITDA multiple element of the sale ($15m). While building Brass Tacks Collective, they had taken the smallest salary possible, enough to pay their mortgage and live. They didn't live to excess. They hadn't taken out much in dividends, either, so they ended up with a big pot of cash at the end. They ended up with far more assets than liabilities: $8 million in assets compared to $2 million in liabilities. The difference was $6 million, which was all theirs as part of the sale of the business. They had built up their cash balance by making a good profit and keeping it, not taking any out as dividends.

Your balance sheet needs to be positive. You need to show that you have the right discipline as a business owner, so you must have healthy fluctuations on your balance sheet that demonstrate that you can manage your business well. Ensure you have efficient operations and good management of assets and cash, just as Hannah and Simon did. With efficient processes, we created systems for faster cash inflows and slower outflows. When you do this, buyers are less likely to find skeletons in the closet when they start doing their due diligence.

🔨 It may be more tax-efficient not to take dividends out of your business before the sale and wrap them up as part of the deal. But the rules on what is most tax-efficient always change, so always speak to a tax advisor or accountant about whether leaving your money in or taking it out as dividends would serve you best.

Treat Yourself Too

It is hard to rock up every day and keep paying people massive bonuses for the performance of the business without seeing any benefit for yourself; that would get really demotivating after a while.

If your numbers say you can afford it, give yourself a little treat each year. Then leave the rest in. Don't go crazy; take out enough to live on, and if you need to take out more every now and then for personal reasons, that's fine. But make sure it is aligned with the growth of your business.

If you take out more, will you be able to hire that new salesperson next year? If you give yourself a big bonus, make sure it doesn't negatively impact another part of your business.

The Holy Grail

The balance sheet is the big picture. This is why Companies House insists on the balance sheets of all companies being publicly available, regardless of their size. This is why it's the key document potential investors will look at if they want to buy your business. It's the document your bank will ask for if you need a loan or need to show even to be approved to work with some suppliers.

Don't ignore your balance sheet. You don't have to plug the numbers in yourself; get your accountant to do that, but get close enough so you can ask the right questions and read a balance sheet like a pro.

Think Like a CFO

Log on to Companies House and pull up some balance sheets of companies that are similar to yours. You will often see two years side by side.

1. Look at the patterns year after year and get an idea of what other companies' balance sheets look like.
2. Highlight bits that catch your attention.
3. Look for patterns: are numbers getting better, or are they getting worse? You can look back over several years and track the changes.

Ask yourself the following questions:

- Is this a positive or negative balance sheet?
- Do you foresee any problems for this company?
- What are they doing well?

🔨 You can do this type of analysis for any company or organisation you're curious about. I looked at the balance sheets for all the schools we considered for my kids. If friends are offered jobs, I look at the employer's balance sheet to make sure they're a stable company to work for. I do it all the time, and it gives you some great market intel!

MINI-CHAPTER:
NEED TO KNOW

THINKING ABOUT SELLING?

If you want to build a business to sell, use **REAP** as a framework to help you plan. (As in, to reap the rewards of building your business.)

1. **R**everse engineer the exit.
2. **E**valuate and enhance value.
3. **A**ttract the right buyers.
4. **P**repare for Sale and Transition.

R – Reverse Engineer the Exit

- Define the **desired outcome**: What does a successful exit look like for you?
- Identify the **ideal buyer**: Are they private equity, a strategic buyer, a competitor, etc.?
- Establish **financial goals**: How much money do you need to walk away with?
- Decide on **deal structure**: All-cash, stock options, earnouts or a mix?

E – Evaluate & Enhance Value

- **Financial Health:** Improve EBITDA, cash flow and financial reporting.
- **Market Positioning:** Strengthen brand, client base and industry reputation.
- **Revenue Model:** Build **recurring revenue streams** to boost valuation.
- **Operational Efficiency:** Reduce reliance on the owner and streamline systems.

A – Attract the Right Buyers

- Profile potential buyers and understand **what matters most to them**.
- Optimise business structure to make it **more appealing and scalable**.
- Expand into **high-value markets** that increase buyer interest.
- Strengthen **key partnerships** that make the business more attractive.

P – Prepare for Sale & Transition

- Get **legal and financials in order**: Contracts, entity structure, tax strategy.
- Conduct a **mock due diligence** to identify and fix any red flags.
- Develop an **owner transition plan**: Ensure the business runs without you.
- Negotiate for the best **valuation, terms and post-sale involvement**.

The time it takes to prepare your business for a sale varies, but I recommend that REAP needs to be done at least two to three years before an exit. Some tax planning work needs to be done five years before, but the actual exit process (once you have an offer from a buyer) can take six weeks or six months, depending on how much due diligence there is to do.

There are different valuation methods across industries. Some would EBITDA, others rely on revenue, and some prioritise the Balance Sheet. Therefore, the price you could sell for could vary, and multiples can be 2-20+.

Do some industry-related research before you start, and https://fullratio.com/ebitda-multiples-by-industry is a useful website. However, you should always get expert advice when planning to sell.

PART 3

GROWING YOUR MONEY

GROWING YOUR MONEY

The Evidence Is in Your Data

There will always come a point when you ask yourself, *Why is this not working?* When you've worked hard towards reaching your business goals, but for some reason, it hasn't worked out. Yet.

This is where your data will help. Think of them as clues to a mystery: you're Sherlock Holmes, and the data you have about your business is your evidence.

In any business, there are areas of data that hold clues to its success or failure, and they can be found in:

- Budgets and Forecasting
- Systems and Policies
- Benchmarking and KPIs

These three areas will help you track and measure your company's financial performance and keep you on your path towards your business goal: your Magic Number.

Like the three financial mechanisms of your balance sheet, cash flow statement and P&L, these three areas also work together to preserve, protect and promote your business:

- **Budgets and Forecasting** → *Protect* → Helps you to avoid overspending and plan for growth.
- **Systems and Policies** → *Preserve* → Helps you to keep your business safe by keeping your data protected.
- **Benchmarking and KPIs** → *Promote* → Helps you to operate within realistic boundaries and ensures you keep growing.

Whether you're reading this to start your own business or you're already running one and want to improve it, understanding how to budget, forecast your numbers and track KPIs can help. They can also apply to areas of your non-business life and will **give you the power to make the right decisions that will move you closer to your business or personal goals.**

After reading this section, you will have the knowledge to predict how well your business is performing and to feel confident in any business decision you make, because you know it will be based on solid data.

It is not enough to know you have cash in the bank or that you're making a profit; it all has to mean something. It has to move you closer to your goals.

So, if you want to make a big impact with your business, read Part 3.

7

———

MAKING YOUR MONEY GO FURTHER

— Budgeting and Forecasting —

We are good at business. The research out there proves it.

Startups with a female founder or co-founders perform 63%[18] better for their venture capitalist investors than those without. Women-founded businesses generally exit faster for *double* the return,[19] and companies with more women in top management positions make 34% higher return on equity and 42% higher return on invested capital. If someone invested £100 and got a 20% return on a male-led company, they'd have £120 back. A female-led business would earn them 34% more, i.e. £161 instead of £120.

This is all compared to companies with the lowest proportion of women in top management positions. We are bloody great.

However, even though the data proves that women are good at business, we still find ourselves at a disadvantage. Women start businesses with 53% less capital[20] than men. We get less funding and have less access to or awareness of funding opportunities. And because we are more risk-averse (or we face more scrutiny and backlash for taking risks[21]), we are less likely to take on loans or make risky decisions that could pay off in the long run.

But knowledge is power. By increasing our financial literacy and our confidence around money (which is what you're doing right now – bloody brilliant), we can begin to destroy those obstacles. We need to figure out how to generate *more* profit with *less* capital and investment than our male counterparts. Not only so we can stick two fingers up to those who criticise, doubt or question us, but so we can have greater success long-term.

Sounds so easy, right? Well, it will be. Knowing how to manage your budget will make you look good and feel more confident about your business decisions. It could potentially help you secure funding further down the line and definitely help you grow your success. When you can talk at length and with confidence about how you've managed your budgets and how you've made smart financial decisions, no one will question how you took a small business idea from your bedroom to a multi-million-pound boardroom.

Can't I leave this budgeting stuff until later?

The simple answer is no.

When I meet new clients, one of the first things I ask is, "Can I see your budgets?" And they always say, "We haven't got any." These are established businesses, and they don't have budgets! Ridiculous. So, I ask, "How do you know if you're achieving what you want to achieve?" "They reply, Well, because we just look at the top line and what revenue we're generating."

Right. Okay, good.

So just pissing in the wind, basically.

A lack of budgeting and forecasting is why businesses fail. Something will inevitably go wrong, and because they haven't planned for it, they don't know how to react. However, if you're always thinking ahead, planning and reacting in a measured, informed way, you'll still get to your goal. It might take you longer than planned, but if you can confidently make a few strategic changes and a few sacrifices, you will feel secure in the belief that you've made the right decision. You *will* achieve your goal (or be within 10-20% of it).

What if I'm more intuitive than strategic?

Being strategic and planning ahead doesn't mean that as a business owner, you have to ignore your emotions or intuition. In fact, a recent study by Leadership Circle[22] found that because female leaders are more likely to have the skills to emotionally connect with people, we are more likely to focus on the bigger picture and therefore be more strategic thinkers. We are more likely to make *balanced* financial decisions. Knowing your budgets and forecasts simply allows you to do what you do best: combine intuition and data to create an informed solution that benefits the entire business.

When To Get Your Head Around Budgets and Forecasts

I promise you it's not as overwhelming as it sounds. If you can manage your personal household budget, you can manage a business budget. However, if you're thinking, I can't even manage my personal budget, let alone a business budget, you should definitely read this chapter. It will help you.

Most businesses won't have an accountant to do this. Most have someone they see once a year to do their taxes, and that's it. That person won't know enough (or care enough) about your business to discover the reality of what's going on. Only you will know whether cutting costs in marketing will have a detrimental impact on new inbound inquiries. Or whether hiring two part-time employees will give you the result you want over one senior employee.

So, until you get a commercial accountant, a CFO or someone whose only job is to look at the whole picture, *you* need to be all over this. Because it's not just about knowing the numbers; it's about how those numbers sit within the business, within the marketplace and against your competitors.

Budgeting Versus Forecasting

How Do I Start Building a Budget?

A budget is fixed. It reflects your plans and goals and outlines your business's expected income, expenses and financial goals over a specific period (e.g. a year).

To start, you need to create a 'base case'. Add up all the costs you need to cover for the year, as well as the non-negotiables. What must be paid for no matter what? Whether your goal is to make two million profit in three years or hire fifty staff, make sure your yearly budgets realistically reflect those goals.

If your business is large, speak to all the departments to find out what they need, too. Does your marketing team need an extra assistant? Do you want to buy more ingredients from your supplier? From there, if you know your goal is to make, say, £50,000 profit this year, your revenue has to cover all those annual expenses as well as leaving enough for profit.

Then you inject some reality into it. Create the same budget where your revenue underperforms by 20%. And another where you overperforming by 20%.

You should have three budgets that give you a good view of what is realistic and achievable. If you overperform or underperform by any more than 20%, I would argue you've done a shit job of creating your budget in the first place. You've either massively undercooked it or massively overegged it, and you need to rethink your spending.

Only do your budget once a year, as it shouldn't change. It should sit there and be a reminder of your original plan for the year.

What About Forecasting?

Forecasting is almost exactly the same thing as budgeting, except it's flexible. It means comparing what you planned (budgets) with what was actually spent and earned, and what is coming (forecasts.)

Say it's June, right now. That means you'd have six months of actual activity to put into your spreadsheet. You also have six months left to do. So you compare your actual spending from January to June with your budgeted spend for the same time period. How close were you? How far off the mark were you? Will you need to reduce your spending in the next six months? Do you need to make some cuts, or has revenue been good? In that case, can you move some budgets around that need it?

You can use these comparisons to create a forecast for the remaining six months of the year. The goal is to review it every month, every quarter or every six months, depending on the needs of your business.

	Forecast - 6 Months Actual, 6 Months Budget				
12 Month Forecast	Actual Results		Budget		Forecast
Example 2	Q1	Q2	Q3	Q4	Full Year
Turnover					
Service 1	531,480	572,141	552,000	552,000	2,207,621
Service 2	339,900	365,904	360,000	360,000	1,425,804
Total Turnover	871,380	938,045	912,000	912,000	3,633,425
Cost of Sales					
Service 1	111,240	119,750	110,400	110,400	451,790
Service 2	71,070	76,507	72,000	72,000	291,577
Total Cost of Sales	182,310	196,258	182,400	182,400	743,368
Gross Profit					
Service 1	420,240	452,390	441,600	441,600	1,755,830
Service 2	268,830	289,397	288,000	288,000	1,134,227
Total Gross Profit	689,070	741,787	729,600	729,600	2,890,057
Expenses					
Staff Costs	220,431	219,340	219,000	219,000	877,771
Marketing	30,000	17,500	24,000	24,000	95,500
Office Costs	54,353	54,084	54,000	54,000	216,437
Professional Fees	11,000	7,500	22,500	22,500	63,500
Other Overheads	72,470	72,112	63,000	63,000	270,582
Total Expenses	388,254	370,536	382,500	382,500	1,523,790
Corporation Tax Provision	57,155	70,538	65,949	65,949	259,591
Net Profit	243,661	300,714	281,151	281,151	1,106,677

Both budgets and forecasts look forward; they both look into the future and plan for what you want to achieve. The forecast just gives you a kick up the ass. It takes that static once-a-year budget and injects a bit of reality into it every six months or every quarter by giving you a revised view of where you're going to land for the end of the year.

If you set yourself a budget and say, "Right, we're going to do five million of turnover and a million of profit," but you get to month three and your best salesperson leaves and takes all your clients with them, what do you do? You re-forecast to take into account that lost revenue. If you still want to hit that million profit, maybe you have to curb the marketing spend or halve the budget for the Christmas party. Look at downsizing the office. When you win a new client, you can forecast again.

Forecasts and budgets work together to help you constantly think ahead and plan. You will never lose sight of that ultimate goal because even with those little environmental and unexpected shifts, you have your plans to keep you on track.

Baking in the Fat

Everyone should bake a little extra fat into their budget. (It's gross, I know. But that's what I call the contingency provision in your budget.) Where you put the fat depends on your business and personal preferences. I prefer to start with wherever the biggest costs are. Look back at your P&L; find where your highest spend is and what that spend is as a percentage of your revenue. Can you do anything to reduce that cost without being detrimental to your product or service?

- For a product business, it's the things out of your control, such as your supplier costs. If they jack up their costs or go bust, that's out of your control. You need extra fat here.
- If you're a service business, your people will be your highest cost, so budget for inflation, bonuses or staff turnover.

Some companies, if they're huge, simply have a 'contingency' line in their budget. If all their costs add up to a million pounds, they might put in an extra £100,000.

I always bake some things into those lines rather than just putting in a flat contingency fee. Then I look at all the smaller costs, like subscriptions, travel, external advisors and ad hoc fees we can do without for a few months. Then, it's staff: are you staffed correctly for the size of your operation? Nobody wants to make redundancies, which is why it's last, but you have to look at the greater good.

Cover as much as you can and know exactly which other areas of the business you can pull money from if you need to. (I call these 'levers': other areas where you can pull a lever and money will be released as needed.)

It is like if the boiler breaks, you need to find the extra cash. You know you spend a lot on food, so you switch from Sainsbury's to Aldi for a few months. Or, you normally drive everywhere, so for the next few months, you get the bus. It doesn't matter which lever you pull; you know what you *can* pull in your household to divert the money towards the boiler.

It is the same with your business. You don't need to do the accounting, but you do need to have an awareness of where there is extra fat you can move around. (Again, sounds gross. Sorry.)

Avoid This Mistake

The one mistake I see many businesses make when budgeting is to forget to take their cash flow into consideration. You might make a brilliant plan, but you still need the means to afford it. Being aware of historical payment patterns and when cash is likely to flow in and out of your business will help you budget effectively.

What If I Get Stuck?

Nobody knows everything, and it's inevitable you'll need help. If you're drowning but you really want to do your budgets, pay someone else to do it. You don't need to hire a financial controller to work for you full-time; just hire a freelance financial modeller every quarter or once a year to update your budgets.

These are financial professionals who can be engaged to develop spreadsheets that map out your business's finances. They can create incredibly useful statements for you. All you need to provide are the inputs: your figures, payment terms and business goals, such as when you wish to hire and what your expenses are.

However, they won't know your business the same way you do; they just work with the data you give them. They won't know about the people you plan to hire and how much they will cost or about your quarterly marketing plans. So you still need to be knowledgeable enough to ask the financial modeller, "What happens if I do this? Can I see what will happen to the cash flow?" Make sure *you* are still on top of your numbers.

Case Study: Lifestyle Business – School Run Studio

James and Michelle's non-negotiables were anything that could free up their time as much as possible. This meant it was very important for them to automate processes to achieve their marketing goals. They needed a budget for a marketing expert, their systems and their automations. From there, we worked backwards: How many courses do we need to sell? How many people do we need in the membership pool? How many private consultations do we need to do?

When you plan your budget, it's important to know the typical spending patterns of your client base and what costs are typical of your industry. Typically, James had a massive dip in December and a peak in January. Michelle had to market and sell more one-to-one client consultations in December to make up for that shortfall. Then, in January, they could take their foot off the gas a bit because everyone was signing up for memberships. There were always different ways they could achieve that goal of paying themselves their Magic Number. Sometimes it required more involvement from them, but we always stayed focused on doing the things that helped them step back from the business.

If you're running a lifestyle business, budget enough to cover your non-negotiable spending: your take-home salary and your dividends – whatever it is you need in your pocket to fund the life you need.

Case Study: Legacy Business – Evergreen Assembly

Whenever you do budgeting, you must start with the goal. What is your goal and how do you achieve it? What is the most important non-negotiable? Whether it's equipment and research or a particular supplier, you need to budget for that non-negotiable.

For this company, it was people and revenue. (As I said earlier, Legacy business tends to focus more on the end game than on how to get there.) But those goals came with a cost. Their solution was to keep hiring more revenue generators: hire two hundred people who all do a million each. Is that realistic? Probably not. While they were completely adamant that they could hire two hundred people in their industry within a few years (which they probably could), it's normal to lose 10-15% of those people every year. So they had to build that in, too. Not only did they have to find all those people, they had to replace the ones that they lost – that brings extra cost. Not to mention the delay between hiring someone and them starting to bring in revenue. They could wait six months for a new employee to bring in their target million.

It is wonderful to have big ambitions and be a big dreamer. A lot of businesses wouldn't be around now if we didn't have people like that. But there's a way to do it without risking everything – including the jobs of the people you employ. If you're running a legacy business, your instinct might be to want to power through. Stay on track. That's what got you to where you are now, right? But without the awareness of your goals and your bigger picture, you're just a bull in a china shop.

Without thinking about their goals, Evergreen Assembly would have continued to look around for people to hire without any real thought about the structure of the business and how a few bad people choices could potentially bankrupt them. As I mentioned earlier, they got a few clients to pay up front, which funded their growth for the next few years. However, as I no longer work with them, I can't say how long that money will last. If it was up to me, I would've slowed the recruitment down and revisited some of their spending choices. Much more sustainable and realistic.

If you're running a legacy business, think about your non-negotiable goal and how you want to get there. Then build everything else around it. Map out your goals; see what's possible and what's not. What alternatives can you try? Maybe it takes you eight years rather than five to get there. Maybe you can buy a smaller company and absorb the department you need. Or change goals and focus on something else instead. There's nothing wrong with pivoting.

Case Study: Business to Sell – Brass Tacks Collective

Brass Tacks Collective were winging it when I first started. I had to sit them down and get them focused. They told me that their Magic Number was $15 million, and they wanted to achieve that number, whether it took five years or fifteen. That was their non-negotiable. This meant that their EBITDA number had to be $3 million per year. Once we knew that, we started budgeting. We looked at the fees we could charge clients versus the costs of each person who generated revenue for the company. We knew that one person could generate X annually, but they cost Y due to support requirements. By closely examining various factors, we figured out our numbers and landed on the number of employees needed to make that profit target.

But that wasn't a number they were comfortable with. So, we pivoted. What other way could this work?

After doing research, we found that the fees we could earn per salesperson were higher in the US than in the UK. So the obvious way to employ fewer people was to focus on the US; less work for more money. Brass Tacks Collective then focused entirely on growing out the US side of the business.

It is important to note that, like all businesses, it's about finding the balance between stability, resilience and a business owner's goals, while also considering personal preferences. For Simon, maintaining a visible presence in Europe was important because it was where the company first started. However, the European office wasn't generating enough revenue; all the profits came from the U.S. A compromise was to keep the operational and finance teams in the UK, where costs were lower, while continuing to support the US office. It was a strategic choice, and it got them where they wanted way quicker than we envisaged.

The One Thing to Focus On

It is impossible to forecast and plan for a million scenarios; we'd never get anything done if we tried. And as luck would have it, the one thing that goes wrong will not be the one you've thought of. If that happens, all your attention goes on surviving and pushing through that experience. You will take your eye off your goal for too long, and when you go back to it, it'll be gone, and you've got to start again.

This is why I'm so pig-headed about knowing what your goal is. If it's to make X amount of profit each year to build up to your Magic Number, *stick to that*. If your budget tells you that you have to wait or make adjustments, you can do it with confidence. You won't ever regret sticking to hitting those numbers.

You always have to sacrifice things in business. But not knowing your numbers should not be one of them. Having your budgets and forecasts done means you know what your options are – where your levers are and where your fat is. So when things do go wrong, it doesn't really matter, because you've planned for it. Whatever it is, you're ready.

Think Like a CFO

Think about the key areas of your business that you spend money on, as these are the areas you need to allocate funds. E.g. marketing, stock, staff.

Write down those three areas where you need to plan your spending and clarify where most of that spend is likely to go. Perhaps most of your marketing spend goes on freelancers, or most of your staff spend is salaries.

What strategy will you use to keep each of those cost lines within budget? What action will you take if the spending gets out of hand?

8

LOGGING ALL YOUR TREASURE

— *Data, Systems and Policies* —

Knowledge is power. It can literally save lives. Caroline Criado Perez's book *Invisible Women* is dedicated to revealing what happens when data on women is overlooked:

- Car crash tests have historically used male-sized dummies, which means women are 47% more likely to be seriously injured in a collision. They are 17% more likely to die.
- Women are more likely to die from heart attacks because doctors aren't trained in spotting symptoms in women, as much of their data comes from male-based data.
- When women's travel patterns aren't considered during town planning (which are different from men's due to unpaid care work and increased public transport use), more women are injured and more severely, too.
- Poorly fitting PPE (largely designed for men due to a 'unisex' approach) means women are more likely to have accidents or be killed, due to protective gear not *actually* protecting them.

This is not to say that we don't lack information on men. There are gaps there, too. But this shows that when we don't have the right information, we build systems that don't work or work against us and slow us down. As women in business, we see a version of this every day. Investors ask us more risk-based questions, while men get asked about their potential for success.[23] Employees put in less effort for female-led businesses,[24] whether consciously or not. And we're more likely to be penalised[25] for our success, especially if we are in stereotypically male-dominated workspaces. So what can we do? Apart from telling the naysayers to shove it, we need to prove them wrong.

We do that with data. With our numbers.

Yes, it all comes back to numbers. It is our evidence. It is the proof that shuts down critics or sceptics and puts you in control of the conversation. The numbers help you run your business logically, not reactively, and grow it better and faster.

Make reliable business decisions by gathering reliable data. Business knowledge isn't just flinging things out and seeing what sticks. That is not research. That isn't data you can make reliable business decisions on. That is just sticking your finger in the air and claiming to forecast the weather. Think about LinkedIn. It has over a billion members across two hundred countries and sixty-seven million company profiles. That is a lot of data. But they didn't get there by accident. Starting in 2002, in Reid Hoffman's living room, they strategically used what they knew about users, company trends, hiring patterns and decision-makers to grow. In 2016, they were bought by Microsoft for $26 billion. Not just because they were a successful company, but because of the data they held about their users.

The insights you have on your clients, your best-selling services, your products and your business are valuable. Even your intellectual property, the ideas and innovative strategies *you* have used to get that business to where it is today are essential. No matter the size of your business, you have valuable data that can tell you how to grow and how to be a success. And that data needs to be logged.

⚖ While it might not be relevant to everyone, if someone wants to buy your company or wants to invest, the insights from your business's data will massively influence its overall value. It drives the value of a company during a sale. Your company's value lies in its data.

What Data Should I Track?

It is easy to get caught up in tracking a million different things that, in reality, don't really matter: how many followers you have or how many people walk through the shop door. It feels good, doesn't it, to know you have thousands of followers on social media? But those are 'vanity metrics'. They don't tell you if your business is *growing*.

The numbers or 'metrics' you need to track are the ones that tell you if you're **making money** and **keeping customers**. Without money or customers, your business doesn't grow. Certain industries, such as technology, have standard metrics that everyone measures, whereas if you're building a professional services business or retail, your metrics will be more individual.

So, what should yours be? What are you measuring right now?

If you've realised you've been tracking vanity metrics, like follower count or email list numbers, that's ok. An ego boost every now and then is good, but it's not a good use of your time and energy. You don't need to track the minutiae of everything. But what should you measure to help your *growth*? I obviously think the best ones are money-related:

- How many leads turn into paying customers? (Conversion rate)
- Money earned from your products or services (Sales revenue)
- What is the rate at which your revenue grows every year? (Revenue growth rate)
- How much does it cost to hire and keep an employee? (Cost per hire)
- How good are your sales and marketing efforts at getting new customers? (Customer acquisition cost)
- How much revenue does every customer generate over their lifetime with your business? (Customer Lifetime Value)

However, depending on your business, you might be interested in metrics that aren't all about the numbers:

- How influential is your business in the market compared to competitors? (Market share)
- How likely are your customers or clients to recommend your business to others? (Net Promoter Score - NPS)
- How many target clients/customers are aware of your business? (Brand awareness)
- How skilled are your staff at generating results? (Employee productivity rate)

You could measure many different metrics, but make sure they are aligned with your business goals. This is why it's so important for you to identify what you're trying to build and who you're trying to build for. Otherwise, you'll just drown in metrics that mean nothing to you. Tracking how long it takes staff to walk from the car park to the office is pointless. As are timed toilet breaks or how much coffee your staff drink. All those things will only make your staff resent you, and it's irrelevant to your growth. It has to be meaningful, such as, "Why did we not win this piece of work? Was it because the client went to a competitor or were we too expensive?" That is useful, meaningful data. Where you met a client for lunch, whether they were late or whether they ordered gluten-free bread is not useful. You've got to hone a handful of really important ones that help you track your **business's progress.** Data holds so much power and value, it drives me nuts that people don't log it properly. It's like running a nice hot bath, then pulling the plug out so the water runs down the drain. Then stepping in. Pointless.

📌 Don't forget: always track your cashflow. Cash is your fuel for business growth, the petrol in your car; you can't go anywhere if it runs out. It funds what you want to do, and the data and the information you track feed the decisions you make about your money.

So, now you know what to track, you need a system to organise and store that information for future business decisions.

How Do I Track It?

We all get a bit forgetful. We all have different recollections of events that have happened. And we are all human. You could say, "Oh, I'll be fine. I'll remember that." But you're not a machine with a perfect memory. And what happens if you go under a bus tomorrow? What if you get sick and can't work? Not logging your data is bonkers. You need hard facts to make decisions from, and if the worst happens, someone else needs to pick up where you left off.

Eradicating the ability for people to make errors in your business is obvious; make business easier to manage, not harder. Therefore, always try to alleviate the burden of responsibility on the person in charge of that task or you as the business owner.

We do that with systems.

When I talk about systems, I'm referring to the processes and equipment you can use to help avoid problems. Once, I got to the end of a year with a sales company, and I asked everyone, "Right, it's commission calculation time. Tell me who is responsible for what revenue out of this $20 million?"

No one could tell me. Soon, the arguments started:

"Well, I did more work on that lead than this one, so I should be getting more."
"Actually, I did more overtime than you."
"You were sick that day. I covered for you, so I should get that."

Without a system to log details of projects, hours, commission splits or client conversations it was impossible to know for sure who had done what. Without logged information, you can't see the bigger picture of how efficiently your business runs.

You also miss key information about relationships. I once worked with a recruitment company where a recruiter had agreed to a fee cap with a client, but forgot to log it. A couple of months later, I sent an invoice to the client, and they came back to me complaining that they'd been overcharged. It took three months, several conversations, a very irritated client, and me looking like an idiot to solve the problem: the agreement hadn't been logged anywhere – only in the recruiter's head. (I'm good, but I'm not bloody psychic!) Ultimately the invoice was sent out late, payment was made late, and our cashflow was buggered up for three months. Reputational damage and problems with cashflow could all have been avoided if everything – all agreements, conversations and context – had been agreed and *recorded*.

If there had been a system for logging that data, it wouldn't have happened.

Systems: An Explanation

We all have systems in our daily lives, so don't assume you can't do this. For example, if you didn't wash your clothes regularly and only did it when you felt like it, what would happen? You'd probably never do it. I wouldn't. Eventually, you'd have no clean clothes left and all the dirty ones would be piled up. It would take days to get through. It would be all over the place, hanging off radiators and on door handles. The tumble dryer would be on constantly, and the place would be a mess.

But with a system for your washing, things are a lot easier. You still have to do it, but it takes a lot less time and is far less of a pain. And you have more clean clothes, more often. It is short-term pain for long-term gain.

A system is about implementing regular, easy processes that help you log and track the progress of your business. There are two types of systems you can use:

- A mechanism or system that records data like an Excel spreadsheet, Google Drive, Trello boards or CRMs.
- Or a collection of workflows that work together to achieve a goal:
    - *a system for getting approvals from senior management.*
    - *systems for logging feedback and improvements about your products.*
    - *systems to create social media posts, marketing strategies, content, videos, market insights and demographics.*
    - *systems to log invoices, due dates, cash flow forecasting, or to run balance sheets.*

Invoice Process Workflow

Sale recorded on CRM → Deliverables completed → Finance raise invoice

Client payment received ← Invoice sent to client ← Delivery team approves invoice

Receipt logged on CRM → Complete

Both types of system log and store data about your business that you can access later to make informed decisions about your business. There are many user-friendly platforms out there that are specifically built for new and seasoned business owners, from Xero to QuickBooks for accounting, and Planable, Buffer or Sendible for marketing. Larger businesses need more complicated systems, and you must research which systems will store the data you need.

Do I Really Need to Create Policies?

Like systems, policies help to prevent people from making mistakes and causing your business to lose money. Having two people sign off on a paycheck or having layers of authorisation are just some examples of policies you can implement to protect your business.

I once made a glorious fuck up where I accidentally paid a bonus to the wrong person. Can you imagine having to say, "Sorry, actually, that bonus isn't for you. Can I have it back?" It didn't take a rocket scientist to work out who the bonus was really for, and how much that person was getting paid.

I worked with another company that had no system or policy in place for making sure they had VAT receipts for their expenses, so they ended up paying more VAT than they needed to. At one point, I had to help them claim back £12,000 of VAT in one year just because of shit expense records. Imagine how much *more* money people are paying to HMRC than they need to, because they don't have a policy for VAT receipts.

Policies don't apply only to finances, either. You can have policies for all sorts of things in your business so your business runs as smoothly as possible. Every business will need different policies, but they generally include guidelines like:

- Expense policies: Can your staff fly business class? Are employees allowed to take clients out for dinner? How much are people allowed to spend on the business card?
- Banking policies: Who is authorised to approve a payment? What do they have to do? How is it logged?
- Marketing policies: Who signs off on a campaign? How do they do that? What happens if something needs to change?
- Sales policies: Who is authorised to do refunds? What happens if someone wants a discount? If a product isn't selling, what is the procedure for feedback and analysis?

Policies will also help to increase the security of your business. I have worked with companies where it could have been so easy to take

£500,000 out of their bank account and no one would have noticed until the money was gone. I have heard of staff accessing the 'Saved Payees' section of a bank account. They change the banking info to their own and make payments through the company as if paying a supplier, but the funds go to them personally. I have had a client where someone clicked on a link they thought was from the bank – and a load of money got stolen.

If those companies had had their policies set up, policies that included secondary approval or software to flag suspicious emails, those mistakes could have been avoided. It is so easy to mistype a number or to accidentally pay the wrong supplier or person. But it's also impossible to monitor everything. Therefore, by implementing policies, you give the people you work with the freedom to do their jobs without worrying about whether or not they're doing it properly. You might think, "Oh, but I trust my staff, I don't need to ask them to follow all these rules." That's great, but this isn't about trust; this is about **protection**. Protect both your business and your staff from the silly mistakes and human errors we all make from time to time.

When you protect your business and its funds with good financial management, you create a resilient business. You want that, don't you? A resilient, strong business that can weather anything from a bad quarter to you falling ill and not being able to work. All the power and information to keep that business running will be in your data, your systems and your policies. Keep them organised, easily accessible and safe.

🪓 There will always be laws, regulations and standards you have to follow when running a business. Not just with money, but with your products, your staff, your locations and anything else related to your business. Make sure you follow the regulations and requirements relevant to your business. When you get to a certain size, you'll have to appoint your own auditor or be audited by an external company. If you don't have the right financial policies and controls in place, your business could have some big problems to sort out.

Work With, Not Against, Your Staff

All these policies could feel very 'Big Brother', and I am not suggesting you implement policies that limit or imply you don't trust your staff. Do not micro-manage or slow their work, but do preserve the value and success of the company, which helps your staff too.

The best policies and systems give people guidelines to work with but still maintain a level of freedom for them to complete it their way. So when asking staff to track and log data, it helps them to understand *why it needs to be done*. What is the benefit to the company, and consequently, to them? For example, why do they need to log all their data about a product launch? Are you going to use it to make the next launch better or are you just tracking their hours worked? If they track how long it takes to make a sale, are you going to penalise them if it takes too long, or are you going to use that data to make improvements?

There's a lot of power, and comfort, in people understanding what's expected of them. If the data feeds all your conversations and decisions, which it should, your staff will very quickly understand and appreciate that what they do is meaningful and adds value. If you audit the processes every month or quarter (or however often is relevant), you can make tweaks to ensure you're always tracking what's relevant and drop what's not.

Just ask yourself what's more uncomfortable: setting expectations from day one and giving people clear guidelines on their processes, or having really difficult conversations when they've not done what you want?

Case Study: Lifestyle Business – School Run Studio

The data School Run Studio had on their clients was great. All their clients signed up online, so everything was stored efficiently in a CRM. They were on top of all their client profiles, their demographics, preferences and habits; all really useful information for how to target people and how to tailor their packages.

But their financial stuff was bloody awful. They had monthly subscriptions they'd forgotten they'd signed up for or expired free trials they were now paying for. They were terrible for not monitoring what they were spending money on or reviewing their outgoings. I remember telling James, "Do you realise how much you spent in coffee shops last month?"

And he shrugged and said,

"It's only a few coffees here and there…"
"Seventy-six quid in one week, James."
"Seventy-six quid on coffees?" "Yes."

Silence.

Then, "Oh, well, yeah. I did buy my client a coffee. Oh, and I forgot I had a bacon sandwich that day, too."

It all adds up so quickly. I am not saying that if you are running a lifestyle business you should never buy yourself a coffee, but tracking your spending will make you more mindful of where the money is going. With School Run Studio, we stripped out all those subscriptions they didn't need and made sure they reviewed their spending regularly.

For Lifestyle businesses, systems and policies are all about cost control and making sure you spend money in the places that give you what you want. If you want to be removed from that business, you need to be very clear on how you expect everyone else to spend the money that you're letting them spend. How do you expect them to go through the process of bringing on a new supplier? How do you expect them to engage with clients? How should they log their data?

Perhaps you've not been involved in the business for several months because you've been travelling or living the life you've created for yourself, but invariably, there will be times that you have to get involved when the shit hits the fan. You will have to come back in and make a decision, but if you haven't been there, and you haven't had all those conversations, you need that data.

Case Study: Legacy Business – Evergreen Assembly

This company had a great system where all the salespeople were supposed to log leads, wins and completions.

But they didn't do it. Or they did it sporadically. Or individuals logged their own work. Or each team created their own spreadsheets and methods for logging.

Information was getting missed. Invoices weren't being sent. Payments weren't being received, and in some cases, they didn't even know cash wasn't arriving. They were still talking about bonuses from the previous year. They were still arguing over who was owed what commission. The amount of time that went into having all those conversations was ridiculous. While I can advise on best practices, it is ultimately the business owner's job to enforce the processes.

When you grow a legacy business, make sure you have a system that records data in a way that everyone can agree on and adhere to, and that provides a single point of data. That means, if you have to check your metrics, you only have to go to one location like a single company database or spreadsheet that everyone uses to record the same information. You shouldn't have to have fifty different conversations with fifty different people to get your answer.

In this kind of business, there are likely to be strong personalities who will not want to track the data, or business goals that don't focus on profit, so you may think, "What's the point?"

The point is, without cash and without logged data, those goals will not be reached no matter how hard you push or how fast you grow – and those personalities risk losing their jobs.

Any successful business, no matter what its goals, needs financial stability. To build stability you need to track that data. Enforce logging data by all your staff, and be crystal clear about what's expected of them. Because if you don't, you risk leaving money on the table.

At some point, you may want investment or a grant, and those organisations will want to know they'll get a return on their investment. If you've got data that shows progress, there's power in that.

⚒ As much as you may have the money to hire a finance team or CFO, they can only work with the data that is recorded by the company and provided to them. If they don't know about a sale or a deal, how do they know to ask questions about it? If that lack of knowledge gets out of hand, all your budgets and forecasts could be wrong and that could mean cash planning is wrong by a million dollars. That is a problem: being wrong by a million dollars on your cash could fold a business overnight. Help your business grow by giving your finance team all the data they could possibly need.

Case Study: Business to Sell – Brass Tacks Collective

People don't buy the people in a business; they just buy the business. If they can access data from a system and not a person, it adds tangible value – multiples – to the exit value. Buyers don't just take ownership of the intellectual property, they buy everything: client lists, suppliers, customer behaviour insights, strategies, past failures and successes and more. That data proves the value of the business. If you have logged data in the right places and not kept it all in your head, your sale value could be worth multiples of five rather than four, a difference of millions in your pocket.

When I started with Hannah and Simon, they had already begun tracking their data, but it wasn't the best system possible. *But it had been tracked.* Whenever we had a dip, we could go back through the data and look at what had changed in our client makeup. Were we doing well because we were getting repeat business or was it from new clients? Were we being a bit slack with our timelines of fulfilling projects?

Due to the nature of their business, Brass Tacks Collective had no recurring revenue, starting from scratch every three months. It was their data that told us we could pivot to the US which is where they found greater and more reliable success. Without their numbers, we never would have known we'd get more revenue there than Europe. This pivot added to their exit value massively, because they could show their track record of repeat business in the US.

If you're building a business to sell, you have an idea of who you want to sell to, or at least the profile of the company you want to target. This means you only need to track and present the data relevant to their interests. We knew that Brass Tacks's buyers wouldn't need a finance or ops team, as they already had one. So, I adjusted the numbers, stripped the cost of a finance and ops team and demonstrated to the buyer the profit number they could expect. Without five years of data to work from, demonstrating the company's value would have been much harder, and they would have ended up with less money. Instead, they actually ended up with a multiple unheard of in their industry.

If you are building a business with the goal of selling it, your data has a very tangible effect on the sale price, as well as affecting negotiations on the smaller things. It will help to answer any questions that come up in the due diligence process and clarify any outliers in your data. If you can't answer why you have peaks and troughs in your records, your exit value risks being a lot lower. The people who come to buy your business will not take your word for it that it's a good buy: they will want proof. And that's in the numbers. Nobody just buys what you're telling them. You have to prove everything.

Sweating the Small Stuff

Depending on your business, the type of data you'll be focused on will be different. No matter what it is, all the activity has to be logged. Whether you're researching medicine, selling coaching programmes or selling brownies, you need to log all your activity so you can see where you're succeeding and where you're bleeding money unnecessarily.

It is so easy to jump headfirst into running a business, thinking about revenue, hiring staff, and doing your marketing, that you can overlook these processes because they're not the sexy part of the business. You can't make a viral TikTok about your expense policies, can you? No one makes a big deal about everyone logging data on a spreadsheet.

But it's the small stuff that makes the big difference. Taking showers instead of baths to save water; not buying coffees every day saves money. It is not the fun and exciting side of things, but it is what makes a difference.

Be clear about what you want to achieve, be honest about it and stick to it. Use your data to make better decisions more often, and you'll get to your destination quicker.

Even if you have no plans to sell, if someone comes knocking on the door and dangles money under your nose, you'll be tempted. It would be stupid not to have all the data ready. You never know.

Think Like a CFO

Start drafting the policies, systems and data you need in your business.

- What financial policies do you need?
- What kind of systems do you need around working with clients or customers, around product delivery or the supply chain?
- What data do you need to track and store, and what can you ignore?
- If someone were to buy your business, could you explain the peaks and troughs?
- If someone were to ask about some unusual spending, could you give them proof as to why you made those decisions?

9

KEEP YOUR FRIENDS CLOSE AND YOUR ENEMIES CLOSER

— Benchmarking and KPIs —

Only 39%[26] of women in the UK are confident in their ability to start a business compared to 55% of men. That needs to change. I don't believe it's down to a lack of ability but rather a lack of knowledge.

Confidence comes from knowledge – from knowing without a doubt that you are moving in the right direction and acting on the data you have. It is human nature to forget where you've come from and to look around and think, "Hmm this isn't where I wanted to be." If you can look back at how far you've come each year, with all the data, facts and numbers, you see that you've actually gone 10% or 20% further than you thought. And that should drive you forward.

If you can see your successes, you can also see your failures. You can learn from them and use them as stepping stones to move faster, rather than as reasons to quit. I believe when you make choices driven by data, you make the right decisions far more often than the wrong ones.

You do that using KPIs and benchmarking. If you've ever driven down a motorway, you've driven over rumble strips that tell you if you're drifting out of your lane or going too fast; you hear the rumbling, and your driving suddenly gets very bumpy. That is data telling you

you're travelling way off course. KPIs and benchmarking are your rumble strips, signs to keep you on the road.

Why Bother With KPIs and Benchmarking?

The bottom line is: business is fucking hard work. So you need clues that tell you if you're doing okay. Little signs that give you the comfort and security you need on those days when things get really shitty. I am not saying you'll never fail if you follow these clues, but you're way less likely to if you check your numbers constantly and understand what they're telling you. When things start to go wrong, you need to be able to look at your numbers and figure out why. If you can't, you won't be able to make those 'savvy' data-driven decisions that are likely to bring you success. Instead, you'll make emotional or reactive decisions that are more likely to come back and bite you in the ass.

KPI: Key Performance or Productivity Indicator

Say you want to drop a few pounds in time for the summer. How do you track your progress? Maybe you get on the scales once a week, or you check whether you can zip up your favourite pair of jeans. When you're really clear about what you're trying to achieve, you can measure your progress. KPIs are units of measurement you can use to check your performance or productivity.

My expertise is in finance, so I focus on financial KPIs, but you should focus on whatever KPIs will help you reach your business goals. Unfortunately, in my experience, most companies don't know what KPIs to track.

So, they track everything. Great.

That's not an efficient use of anyone's time. There is no point in tracking seven hundred KPIs if they do not answer a single question about whether your business is heading towards your goal. You could measure every single metric on the planet, but if it doesn't tell you that you are capturing the European market (if that's what you want to do), or that you're growing your online sales, why the fuck are you looking at it?

If it doesn't answer the question, "Am I heading in the right direction to achieve my goal?" then it's not strategic, and it's a waste of your time.

Which KPIs to Track

Pick a handful of really good ones and ignore the rest. Five to ten at most.

That's it. If you're flapping around wanting to get big results in six months, and you're looking at fifty different KPIs, worrying about marketing, and worrying about where the cash is coming from, you will drive yourself up the fucking wall.

You can't possibly be everything. You can't do everything, no matter how much you wish you could. You have to hone in on what's important to your business goals and ignore the rest.

So, what would you track?

Example 1: If your business goal is to earn £100,000 per year in revenue from your online business, you could track:

- → What is your monthly revenue, and is it growing?
- → Are your sales growing month on month?
- → How often do you get repeat sales from the same customer?
- → What is your online engagement rate?

Example 2: If you wanted to eventually work yourself out of the business so it could run without you, you could track:

→ What is your monthly revenue, and is it growing?
→ What is your profit margin with and without you in the business? (Profit / Revenue x 100)
→ How much profit per product/service do you make?
→ Is the revenue *you're* producing decreasing each year? (It should be going down if you want to be less responsible for revenue generation over time.)
→ Is the revenue each employee makes increasing?

Example 3: You want to branch out into Europe.

→ What is your profit margin by region?
→ What is your revenue growth rate by region
→ How many clients do you have in the UK vs Europe?
→ What is your brand awareness in Europe?

🔖 Many financial KPIs remain the same for most businesses, because a business cannot run without cash. After that, prioritise the KPIs that get you closer to your business goals.

You can always change your KPIs as your business grows and changes, but don't do so until you have at least six to twelve months of data first. That way, you can account for seasonal fluctuations in customer behaviour and other external factors out of your control.

Benchmarking: Talking to People

This is when you take those KPIs and compare them to a competitor's or the industry standard. It is like when you go on holiday, and you're unsure if tipping is expected or just something tourists do, so you watch what everyone else does and make a decision based on that. You use the information from businesses in your industry to inform your own business decisions.

So, where do you start? You start with your CAR. Your CAR will get you to your destination:

C: Compare
A: Assess
R: Reality check

1. Compare

Compare five or six businesses as similar to your business as you can find, and find out what their KPIs and results are. You could use an internet search to tell you what the average social media engagement rate is for a company like yours or how long it should take you to convert a client, but you'll get better and more up-to-date information by immersing yourself in networks and talking to other business owners about what their KPIs are. What questions could you ask them? Things like:

- What are their averages for what you want to measure?
- How long do their staff spend on revenue-generating activities?
- What is their client retention rate like?
- What is a normal amount of time for achieving a goal?
- What should the average utilisation rate be for team A?

Scribble down the kind of questions you'd want answers to.

Do I Have to Network?

Yes. You probably already do it, you just don't call it 'networking'. Men have historically benefited from 'the old boys network' taking advantage of who they know to build businesses: people they went to school with, worked with or friends of friends. Women have the same. Women are just as good at starting communities and sharing opportunities with each other; we just don't call it 'networking', but that's what it is.

I know having to go to events to meet other people will still fill some readers with dread. But there are alternatives: online forums, online communities, groups and servers where you can ask questions and share information. Do not underestimate other entrepreneurs: people like to help people, and women do want to help each other. We just need to start having more open conversations around business and money. When you do, you'll find many will be quite open about sharing snippets of information. While they won't necessarily go into details about how much profit they're making, they'll be happy to share what percentage profit they're making on their revenue or what their average fees are.

The dreaded 'networking' isn't always about being in rooms and making small talk; it's about being on the right platforms and asking the right questions. I am part of a recruitment-specific finance network (it's just finance people who work in recruitment). I often share tons of anonymised information, and I get snippets of information in return. It has been incredibly valuable. There is power in shared knowledge.

2. Assess

Eventually, you will get a decent range of data with numbers that vary between 10%-20% of yours. Like:

- The average profit margin was 5% lower than you hoped it would be.
- The average time to convert a customer is actually 12% longer than you thought.
- The average customer retention rate was 3% higher than you thought.

To decide if you are comfortable falling into that range, apply your own logic and goals to the information. But you can use this information to start making good business decisions.

When You're Not Performing: An Example Scenario

What happens when you get your data and realise that your revenue is way below the industry average? What do you do?

Don't panic. Use it to make a business decision:

1. Your business goal and mission is to give employment to one hundred single mothers and have a revenue of £2 million. You could decide that for the first few years, you are ok with falling under the average, because you're still building, but by year five, you want your average revenue to be in the middle of that range, as you want to be able to pay your staff above the market rate.

2. You could decide that you don't want that. You want to grow faster. So, you automate what you can and adjust staff hours and responsibilities. You also take on some of the marketing and admin work yourself. Then you review where you are after eighteen months.

When You're Performing Too Well: An Example Scenario

What if you review what you find, and discover you're making a profit margin of 50%, whereas everyone else is making 30%? Does that mean you're winning? Time to break out the champagne?

Sorry, no.

You need to stay objective. Why is there such a huge variance from the industry norm? To me, that suggests:

1. Costs are too low or you're selling your soul.
2. You are overcharging clients, and at some point, they'll realise and leave.
3. You could be underpaying and overworking your staff.

See if you've overlooked anything in your numbers. While we all want to perform better than our competitors, we have to be objective and make sure it's not at the expense of our staff or customers.

This is a really powerful position to be in, to be able to make those kinds of decisions with confidence. That is a level of control over the future of your business that many other people don't even think about, let alone realise they can do.

3. Reality Check

Other businesses' KPIs shouldn't be your goals. Focusing on upper ranges can be misleading, as there are always reasons for the answers found:

- A competitor's monthly costs are lower than yours. **Reality:** they invested in a massive piece of tech two years ago that cost a fortune, and therefore, they are cutting costs now to save money.
- A competitor only uses a premium ingredient in their product. **Reality:** their favourite supplier went out of business, but it would cost more to source from abroad. Their best choice was a local premium supplier.
- A competitor makes double your profit margin. **Reality:** they're underpaying their staff.

There will always be reasons for what your competitors do, so apply some subjective reasoning to their numbers and dig around into why their profit margins or costs are the way they are. Think of it as a recipe to tweak or a template to adapt. It is useful to see what everyone else is doing, but you have to adapt it to make it your own.

These are not business tools to use to beat yourself up. Stick to your own lane and focus on your own business goals, but always be aware of others. Remember, investors and lenders want confidence. When you know your numbers, you prove that you have potential for growth and success. Own those numbers.

Some Final Tips

1. Don't use crap data

Benchmarking and KPIs rely on data. If you run off crap data, it'll give you crap outcomes. There is absolutely no point in running a load of KPIs and yelling at people for not hitting targets if what you're basing it on is incorrect. Make sure the data is correct.

2. Don't choose too many KPIs

The biggest mistake people make is to get bogged down in too much data. Looking at these KPIs is a massive time commitment because if something doesn't match up, you have to dig into why that's happening, which can be a lot more time-consuming than you think. You could lose weeks or months trying to figure it out. Be deliberate about which ones you'll focus on. They have to be worth the effort.

3. Take comfort in your numbers

When Covid appeared in 2020, nobody had ever experienced anything like it. It impacted a lot of businesses heavily, and no one knew what was normal. Many of the normal KPIs and metrics businesses used to check whether they were running well changed drastically. By benchmarking against competitors and comparing KPIs, business owners were still able to see what everyone else was doing, and that added comfort to a very unpredictable and difficult time. Knowing they were operating within the same boundaries as everyone else, even with those environmental impacts, added a sense of security.

Case Study: Lifestyle Business – School Run Studio

When I joined School Run Studio, James and Michelle had been benchmarking against competitors in terms of pricing and product offerings. They had also tracked client retention rates as a KPI, using it to adapt their business to seasonal fluctuations between the summer and winter. When I started, I suggested we begin tracking revenue and profit margins more closely, and KPIs related to client-facing work: how happy are the customers? Would they buy it again? Are they getting repeat client business? Feedback from your customers gives you valuable new information that will help your business grow.

They also had KPIs related to their marketing manager. As they wanted minimal involvement in the company, she was brought in to do their social media as well as manage the community and deal with customer queries. She was important, so I suggested we switch to making sure she was giving them a good ROI. That means tracking

KPIs to measure whether she was generating new business. It sounds gross because it makes her sound like a piece of software, but we had to track the ROI of their investment in her. The results showed she was answering 98% of customer questions without having to refer to James or Michelle, and she answered them correctly, which showed that she was knowledgeable. Customers liked her, and she was good at her job. It was a good ROI.

If you're running a lifestyle business, there are key KPIs you should always track:

- Revenue growth over time.
- Revenue per client.
- Profit margin.
- Profit as a percentage of revenue.

If you're bringing on staff so it can eventually run on its own, many of your KPIs will be related to them:

- Customer satisfaction.
- How efficient they are at answering questions.
- How often they have to ask you questions.

If your business is highly automated, your KPIs should measure the efficiency of the software:

- Do people like using it?
- Would you get better work out of a human?
- Does it sell well enough or fast enough?

Case Study: Legacy Business – Evergreen Assembly

Their goals were growth and increasing their headcount. While they were on track to meet their revenue and people goals, they were unaware of the underlying issues. Looking at their KPIs for profit, I could see that their profit margins were too small because they were spending too much money on things that didn't matter. They were overspending on office space and on staff. In their industry, it's normal to spend somewhere between 40% and 60% of revenue on your staff, including all bonuses and extras. They were spending

75%. They wanted to pay 10% above the market rate, because they wanted to attract the best salespeople. That made sense for a 10% difference, but not 15%. When I looked at it, I found problems in the way commissions and bonuses were awarded. Not a massive issue on the surface, but if it went on too long, the company would run into trouble, and staff would start getting upset.

They were also looking at really detailed operational KPIs: How much time do people spend on the phone? How good are they at logging their data? How quickly do they fill jobs? How many CVs are they putting in front of clients? They were tracking all these internal metrics, but it wasn't clear why they were tracking that data.

Data accuracy and data logging were a big problem. Their KPIs and benchmarking were much harder to manage because the data being used was inaccurate. While I could advise as their CFO, ultimately it was the founders' decision to continue as they were.

If you're running a legacy business, you have to be incredibly strict and enforce good habits and behaviours around logging data. You need to have crystal clear KPIs and benchmarks, and refer to them regularly. Without those, you won't have the data you need to efficiently reach your business goals.

Case Study: Business to Sell – Brass Tacks Collective

Simon and Hannah had to monitor the KPIs that would increase their exit value. One of them was to have a strong brand, so that meant saying no to certain jobs that would dilute their brand reputation. Another was to increase their revenue to a point that would be attractive to buyers.

So, we decided to make the average fee per client a KPI. By tracking the average fee Brass Tacks could charge in Europe versus the US over two years, we found that the US market was more profitable: more fees for less work.

Once we had focused on the US, we added other KPIs, like how much time staff spent on business development calls to the US versus

Europe. We didn't care about the overall amount of time; if they spent seven hundred hours on business development calls, fine. We just wanted the ratio of US to European calls because that's where we wanted to grow the business.

We also benchmarked against other similar businesses in the US and realised we were charging about 3% less than the average, so we upped our prices. The market didn't react, and the business moved forward towards more profit. There came a point at which they were making almost 60% profit margin, completely unheard of in that industry. Instead of celebrating, we realised it wasn't sustainable. Yes, it was great that we were making all this money, but it meant that people were overworked and they didn't have enough support. At some point, someone was going to crack and that would have a completely opposite effect on the business. So we had to think about making more hires and investing more cash or better systems to help people do their jobs.

Think Like a CFO

Get in your CAR and start getting the data you need to benchmark your business against others.

Write down what you find and keep it somewhere safe; you'll need to update it regularly.

Then, think back to your Magic Number. What was it?

What five to ten KPIs do you want to measure to help you get to that number?

Write them down and stick to them. Do not change them for at least six months, when you can review and reassess.

10

TAXES ARE FUCKING COOL

— *Compliance and Tax* —

Let's face it, we all have a slightly unhealthy, needy, co-dependent relationship with our business. Whatever we do in our personal lives affects it. And whatever happens in our business affects our personal lives. You are connected. Intertwined. You can't untangle yourself no matter what.

But people forget that their money is also interlinked. Your business pays your salary. Your salary determines how much you have to work. How much you work determines your revenue. This pays your salary, and round the circle goes.

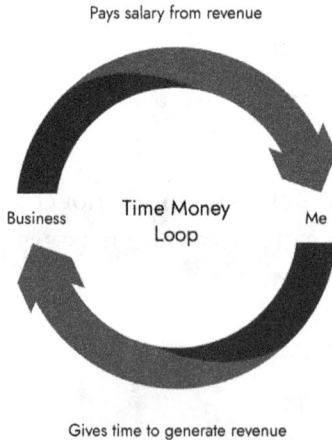

Pays salary from revenue

Business   Time Money   Me
                      Loop

Gives time to generate revenue

And then there are your taxes, just as interlinked and tangled in your personal and business life. If you experience some anxiety because this is the first time someone told you this, it's not your fault.

School was shit at preparing us for this reality. We never learned about taxes or how to manage our money, but we know that Pythagoras liked triangles and Henry VIII had six wives, two of whom he beheaded. (Is there a reason we need to know that?) No wonder we are so rubbish with money and we bury our heads when it's tax time. Knowledge is power, but what is the lack of knowledge? Fucking stressful, that's what. No matter how much you dig into and think about what that tax pays for, no one wants 20-50% of their pay taken away in tax. It hurts. Whatever level you're at, it hurts. To avoid that stress, we tell ourselves we'll think about it later. We all just want an easier life. "Tax doesn't need to be taxing," says the advertising strapline. But *it is* taxing. I'm an accountant, and I hate tax. It is genuinely quite frightening because you don't want to get it wrong. If you do, you end up with a fine – or worse. It is the most complex niche area of accountancy, and there is no getting away from that.

But there are benefits to getting on top of this stuff. The biggest benefit is that you could end up with *more* money in your pocket, not less. But if you don't figure it out, that won't happen. You need to learn how to hold on to as much of your money as possible. A lot of people get all kinds of high and mighty about this, saying, "We should all be paying our taxes," and I agree. I am talking about how to *avoid* paying more tax than you have to, which is legal. It is tax *evasion* that is illegal.

→ **Tax avoidance** is when you use legal methods to reduce your tax bill. (It could probably have a better name, if we're honest.)
→ **Tax evasion** is when you know there is tax to pay, and you just don't. You commit fraud, and you hide information.

This chapter won't teach you how to become a tax accountant or how to avoid tax. I am not a tax expert. I would never touch a company tax return in a million years. But I am a bloody good CFO, and what

I will do is teach you how to think differently about taxes so you can ask the right questions and avoid paying too much. But to ask the right questions, you have to know a bit about accountants first.

Do You Speak £$€?

Accountants speak a very different language from most people, full of complicated and very boring financial terminology like 'amortisation of intangible assets' or 'EBITDA' or 'normalisation adjustments'. You probably switched off reading that sentence. Welcome back. They forget that regular civilians don't speak 'accountant'. That means you need a translator. Many larger businesses have a financial expert such as a Financial Director or CFO, who can be that financial translator, helping leadership and finance teams work together to achieve a common business goal. However, most small businesses and start-ups won't have someone like that yet. Until then, they've got to be able to talk 'accountant'. Like any language, it comes with its own traditions and cultural expectations.

1. Accountants Won't Think For You

Once, back in 2024, I was working for a company and received a reminder from HMRC saying I hadn't filed a tax return for the business. I knew we had. In fact, I'd hired an external company to do our taxes because I wanted to keep my work separate from the taxes of the business.

I ignored the reminder. I told myself that HMRC was just sending out their usual automated reminder and had simply forgotten to update their records. A few weeks later, I got another reminder saying our company accounts hadn't been filed. And we'd been fined. Great.

When I went to check, it turned out they *hadn't* been filed. It transpired that the external company I'd hired had been partway through doing the taxes when I told them, "We're switching to a new provider this year. These will be the last you do for us." As the new provider wanted all the financial information, I offboarded the old one. What I didn't realise – much to my fury – was that as soon as the offboarding was done, the older provider just downed tools and didn't complete the filings.

I lost my shit. Hadn't it occurred to them to inform me that they would stop work after the offboarding? If I had known I would have waited.

No, it did not occur to them. It was not their problem. This is a prime example of people not giving a shit if they don't have to. They do their jobs, and nothing more.

You could argue that it is their job to inform you of these things, but in reality, it's not. They don't do things that way in the accountancy world. Their job is to do the financial paperwork and advise you of issues that could come up based on what you give them. If you ask their advice based on specific information, they will answer. But they have no incentive to give you any more than they have to. It is not their responsibility to think about the impact on the business – it's yours.

You have to be on top of this shit even though it's boring. You don't have to do it yourself, but you've got to make sure it's done and done correctly. Just because you pay someone to do your taxes for you doesn't mean you avoid responsibility for those numbers. You are still the business owner or director. It is still your legal responsibility to make sure that certain boxes are ticked when it comes to tax and compliance. If you don't, and you sign your name to their work, you are the one who will pay the fine or get struck off.

2. The Yearly Moment of Dread

Tax comes around every year. Like Christmas, it's an expensive time of year. Create a little routine, a tradition if you like, of tucking money away for taxes. Create pots or open extra bank accounts to save money for your corporation tax, VAT and your personal tax bill. It makes the pain of paying taxes a little easier. It sounds like a small thing, but it's transformative. You don't ever have to worry about a looming tax bill because it'll be covered. If you have some left over after you've paid your tax, go and spend it, have a nice little jolly.

However, you can budget all you want, but if you don't tell your accountants everything, things go wrong.

School Run Studio relied on an external accountant for all their company filings and personal tax returns. One year, while James and Michelle were in New York on holiday, their accountant sent them their tax bill, and it was £1,000 less than they were expecting. So they thought, "Right! Let's go shopping!"

It transpired that the accountant had forgotten to include rental income they earned from their flat – and they hadn't reminded him of it. By the time they realised, they'd already spent the extra cash. They then had to come up with another £1,000. It was no one's fault, just a classic story of something getting missed.

Putting aside money into pots for taxes eliminates the worry and that's what I advised James and Michelle to do. If James had a month when he couldn't put the aside money, he'd ring me to ask, "I'm £200 short, what do I do?" And I'd talk him through it. "Got any outstanding invoices?" "Yeah, someone hasn't paid yet." "Okay, as soon as that comes in, put the extra £200 away. Don't stress about it."

So, how much to put away?

As an individual running a limited company, you have to pay business taxes and personal taxes. Below are some suggested amounts to set aside to cover those taxes. They are not the exact amounts you'll have to pay, just a suggestion to make sure your bills are covered.

Business Tax

- **Corporation Tax** → based on your operating profit. (This is your profit after costs have been deducted but before tax.) The rate you pay will depend on which tax band you fall into. Aim to budget 25%, but governments can change this at any time.

- **VAT** → If you have reached the VAT threshold, you need to put away 20% of your sales invoices for that too. You will be able to recover some of the VAT you've paid on your costs, but if you put away 20% of your revenue, you'll have more than enough.

Personal Tax

- **Income Tax** → The most tax-efficient way for a director of a company (you) to pay themselves is to take a basic salary topped up with dividends. You would pay a very small amount of income tax on the salary (if any), and there are minimal additional costs to the company for that salary.
- **Dividend Tax** → depends on how much you take out across the year. Again, there are bands depending on how much you take. I recommend putting away 32.5% of what you pay yourself as dividend tax.

In any business, it's important to show business growth and balance sheet resilience whilst also maximising your own tax advantages. It is a massive balancing act. If you want to build a resilient business or you are planning to sell, you need a strong balance sheet. You need reserves (i.e. a pot of cash made up of profits from previous years). Wiping out all the profit to avoid corporate tax could be counterproductive. Speak to a tax advisor who can help you find the right balance based on your business type and goals.

If you can't afford to put money aside for your tax bill, that tells me you can't afford what you're doing. The tax bill <u>always</u> needs to be paid. If you haven't got enough cash to put away, you're overspending or you need to make changes to create better cashflow. If you can't save enough in one month, top it up the next month. If there's a late invoice, stay on top of it. You will sleep better at night knowing your tax bill is covered.

Separation of Business and Personal

In some cultures, there are traditions that don't make sense to people outside of that culture. For example, when we are stuffing the turkey for Christmas dinner, we spank the turkey. (I know it sounds like a disgusting euphemism, but I promise it's above board!) The tradition doesn't make sense, but it's how we do things. So, even though your personal and business finances are inextricably linked, tax accountants won't see it that way. It is just not how they do things, either. You will have a personal tax accountant and a corporate tax accountant, and they'll treat their jobs very separately, but one will always affect the other. It is swings and roundabouts. If you're a shareholder or director of a company, there are always things you can tweak on one side that mean better outcomes on the other side and vice versa. Always ask yourself and your accountant:

How does that impact me as a person?
How does that impact my business?

Most people make the mistake of putting personal things through the company that they shouldn't, assuming no one will ever find out. It is true that the risk is low of HMRC ever coming knocking, saying, "We think you're being cheeky with your expenses." But be aware of the risk. You could put something through that flags your account to HMRC. If you ever want to sell a business, you could come unstuck.

Simon, at Brass Tacks Collective, had bought a house for his son through the business by taking a personal loan from the company. All perfectly legal. But because it had a residential element to it, even though he wasn't living in it, it should have been declared as a personal benefit. He should have paid personal tax on it. It was missed by the external accountants, and when it came to selling, it came up in due diligence as a reason to reduce the price of the sale: the buyers wanted to reduce the sale price by £100,000. Luckily, we were able to correct the mistake in time and pay HMRC what was owed, and it wasn't an issue. But that was a lot of stress that could have been avoided.

Ask Questions and Communicate

There are always better ways of managing your finances, but you have to ask the right questions, and you have to be open with your accountants: tell them everything. There is no such thing as giving too much financial information to a tax accountant because the more they have, the more they can analyse the numbers and help you. When one of Evergreen Assembly's business owners moved from the UK to the US, they took some tax advice about a very clever tax mechanism: if you have a UK company making losses, you can offset those losses against your personal tax in the US. What nobody explained to them – because they didn't ask the question – was what happens if that UK company begins to make profits? You have to pay tax on that profit in the US as a person. No one told them it works both ways. If you make a £100k profit in the UK, you have to add that to your £200k of US income and pay tax on the total amount.

To offset a loss means using a business loss (when you have more expenses than revenue) to reduce your taxable income. If your UK company loses £200k and your personal income in the US is £400k, you can subtract the £200k loss from your £400k income. This lowers your taxable income to £200k, reducing the tax you owe.

Income Source	UK Company	US Personal	Total
Personal Income		400,000	400,000
Profit/Loss	-200,000		-200,000
Taxable Income			200,000

Overall income is less, so less tax is paid

Tax accountants won't answer the questions you don't ask. So always ask *all* the questions. Don't hold it in. Don't be shy. Play dumb if you have to. But go to them and ask, "This is what I'm doing in my personal life. I'm spending this. In business, I'm doing this. What's the most tax-efficient thing I can do? Tell me everything. What should I know?"

Talk openly about what you earn and spend, and how that money moves around your business. It is not an accountant's job to judge you for what you do. I can guarantee they've seen worse.

Tax Responsibilities to Watch out For

Tax is a big and complicated topic, and the tax you have to pay depends on your business's circumstances. However, there are some tax responsibilities almost all business owners should know about, no matter their size.

1. You have to pay tax on any interest you earn in a business account. Tell your accountant.
2. The most tax-efficient way to pay yourself is to take the minimum salary and top it up with dividends. But if you don't earn enough profit in a tax year to take those dividends, the shortfall is considered a 'director's loan', and you have to pay tax on that loan. Keep an eye on your profits and make sure that you don't take too much out each month. Otherwise, set aside a bit of extra tax to cover that amount.
3. If you're moving money between countries, say exchanging dollars into pounds, you will gain or lose money on it depending on the timing and the rates you get. You are not allowed to do that for the sole purpose of making money. But if you do make money, you have to pay tax on it.
4. If you put a cost through the business that isn't for your business use, e.g. a car, you have to pay tax on it.

There are so many other examples to look out for, but it would be overwhelming to list them all. However, most gains/losses will have some sort of tax/ tax allowance, so tell your accountant everything! If it's not a business cost, tell your accountant, anyway. Ask them to help you understand the most tax-efficient way of doing things. Accountants love saving tax, so don't be shy; the more info you share, the better.

Tax Is Your Responsibility, Not Your Accountant's

You have to be on top of this shit. When your accountant asks you to sign the files to confirm they are correct and a true reflection of your business, you have to know that what you're signing is correct. Otherwise, you could be putting your name on a shoddy bit of work that will cost you more than you realise.

I know it's boring. But it's the most expensive boring thing to get wrong.

Can I really do this?

If you're clever enough to start a business, you're clever enough to grasp tax. You are reading this book right now, which proves you're no idiot. You don't have to know everything about taxes, but you do have to manage and plan them, just like no one else is going to make you quit smoking or go to the gym; *you* have to do that. Take responsibility. Even if you ignore your taxes and save them for a time when you have more energy to deal with them, HMRC and Companies House won't. They have the power to freeze your company and hold all its assets. You can't trade. You can't do a thing. If a client pays you, it bounces back. If you attempt to pay suppliers, the payment fails. They hold your assets until you get everything up to date.

I fully empathise with how complex and scary this can be, and it's not about being able to do your taxes on your own. I don't do everything myself: I have a cleaner, I have someone creating the graphics for this book, and I have someone building my app. It is about managing what needs to be done and making sure it happens, because ignoring it does not make it go away. Accept the responsibility of learning about and understanding your taxes. It's what is expected of you as a company director. Set up a call with your tax accountant now and start asking questions. No one else is going to do it for you.

Think Like a CFO

Let's think about how your personal tax and your business tax are interconnected.

Create two columns on a piece of paper.

In one column, write down every element from your personal life that creates a tax burden, e.g. salary, dividends, rental income, childcare benefit.

In the second column, write down every element of your business that creates a tax burden, e.g. profit, selling assets, paying salaries.

Mark down in the two columns where there is overlap between personal and business.

For example:

1. More profit for the business means more corporation tax.
2. It also means more profit for you to take as dividends, which means more personal tax for you to pay.

PART 4

MONEY X PEOPLE = PROFIT

MONEY X PEOPLE = PROFIT

As much as it would be amazing to build a business alone without having to rely on anyone else, you can't scale without help. You can't be in twenty places at once and you can't make all the decisions. You would fall apart.

You need to hire the right people. Not only that, you need to hire them at the right time.

Finances and HR overlap a lot; therefore, CFOs and FDs will naturally have a decent amount of knowledge in the area of HR. We spend a lot of time working with business owners about where best to use their funds, and hiring decisions play a massive part in that. Before you hire someone, you have to ask yourself:

Will this person bring more money into the business?
Do they align with the culture of the business?
Can the business afford this person's costs?

Your numbers can be positively or negatively affected by the people you choose to hire, especially if you plan to exit, as a successful sale is determined by the business culture and the people you have.

A lot of my previous roles have had a broader remit than finances, so I've been fortunate to have worked across HR, ops, legal and IT. A lot of my clients have been in the staffing and recruitment industry.

I know about the relationship between people and money.

In Chapters 11 and 12, you will learn how to approach hiring people as it relates to your money, and you'll be able to spot whether someone is a good hire for your business.

Then, in Chapters 13 and 14, I will share my insights on working with investors and finding funding. A lot of my work is about preparing a business for investment or sale, and as usual, it's all about getting the numbers right. So, whilst I can't advise you on how to approach an investor, I can prepare the groundwork for you. Investors are also people you work with, and like hires, they have a direct impact on your business.

Even if you don't ever plan to hire or work with investors, choosing not to work with them is still a conscious business decision. So read the next four chapters with an open mind. Arm yourself with the knowledge of what is possible, whether you choose to go down that path or not.

11

IT TAKES A VILLAGE

— *People and Teams* —

It takes a village to build a business. I don't think I realised how true that is until I started building my own. When I'd barely even begun, I roped in several people to help with content creation, video editing, animation, app development and course creation. I am very aware of my own limitations of skill and time, and whilst I love knowing and understanding everything about my work, I know that if I don't loosen the reins, I'll never achieve anything.

You can't do everything and be everything and do it well. Yes, we can have it all, but we can't do it *alone*. We need help. Specifically, operational help. We need to hire the right people.

Who Are the Right People?

Very often, companies are good at rewarding salespeople because they bring money in. We get seduced by the exciting work that sales, marketing and business development do. But it's a mistake to assume that only revenue-generating employees are valuable. You can have incredible people who don't bring a penny in but are just as important, and who bring in value you don't see and can't measure. People who work in operational roles are those people. They take care of bloody important yet boring stuff that no one talks about. They go in, do the work and get out: they are the unseen and unsung people of business. Just like stay-at-home partners who support the ones bringing home the money, people in operational roles lighten the load for business owners and positively impact profitability:

- Accountants help you manage your money so you can make a profit and don't go bust. They can be hugely impactful in managing foreign exchange losses, tax burdens and guiding your overall strategy.
- HR help keep your staff productive and happy and protect your business from employment law issues.
- Admin staff speed up and streamline processes and take the headache out of everyday tasks.
- Logistics optimise deliveries and stock, increasing customer satisfaction and preventing you from spending cash unnecessarily.
- IT help growth through automation, security and data and protect your business and data from breaches and legal claims.

They are the glue that holds it all together, and companies don't understand how valuable a good operational employee is until they're gone. My advice is not to underestimate those critical people or undervalue what they do. They make your life easier and your business more efficient.

🗡 If you're planning on selling your business, buyers won't just look at profitability: they will check efficiency too. You need good operational staff if you want to sell for a higher number.

Who Should I Hire?

When and who you hire depends on where you are in your business. If it feels like you've hit a plateau and you want to go to the next level of growth, that's a good time to start hiring. As this book is all about financial literacy, let's talk about accountants. Exciting, I know.

Just as different types of lawyers specialise in different areas of law, there are different, specialist types of accountants.

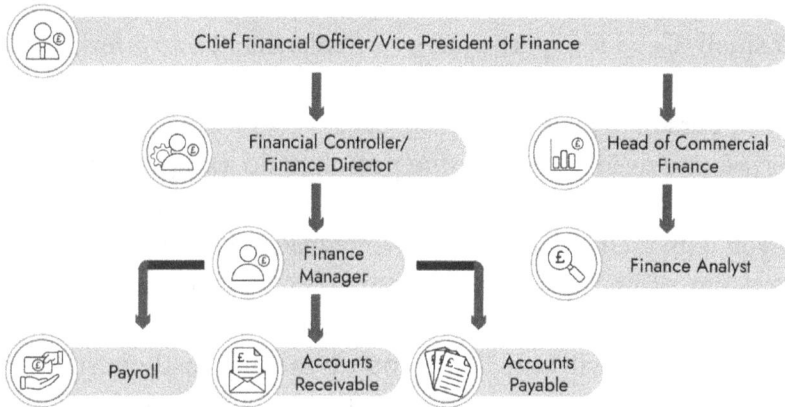

I am a commercial accountant, so when a client hires me, my whole focus is on the growth of the business and how to help it achieve its goals, but I'm not going to chase anyone for invoices or do your payroll. I couldn't do your tax returns. Well, I probably could, but it would be an absolute disaster. If you're a business of one or a start-up, a bookkeeper is usually enough. They can do the basics and will be good at record-keeping and number crunching, but don't ask them for strategic business advice. Accountants all have specialities and levels of expertise, so hire the right person for the right role. Then, as your business grows and the pressure starts to weigh on your accountant or bookkeeper, that's a sign to start expanding and hiring where there is the greatest need in your business.

If you'd like to see a breakdown of all the different types of accountants and financial experts you could hire, there's a resource at the end of this chapter. It lists the roles and responsibilities of each type of accountant. It also tells you the size of business you would expect to find them in. Use the resource to start planning who you'll need to hire.

What if I Can't Afford It?

Start small. Get a few part-timers or freelancers to do a few days a month, then increase their hours or go full-time as needed. Do not hire one person to do all the work, because you won't get the niche expertise you need. Why hire one person to do a crap job of several things, especially if money is tight. Imagine hiring a bookkeeper to help you with your records and then crowbarring them across several other departments, from IT to Finance to HR and a few others, just to save some cash. That person will be unqualified and uninterested in those roles. They will hate it and end up making costly mistakes or quitting. It is like hiring an accountant and asking them to do your legal contracts for you. It doesn't make sense. Hire experts ad hoc instead of one full-time generalist; it's a no-brainer.

Hire People, Not Skills

At the time of writing this book, the UK job market is crap. Unemployment is up, and job vacancies are down. So, there is way more competition for jobs, which puts any business looking to hire at an advantage. But having the right person in a job isn't necessarily about their qualifications or their experience anymore. My best working relationships have been those in which I've been hired for the person I am; expertise and strategic financial advice, as well as a good personality fit. Transparency is essential to my work, so business owners need to feel comfortable talking to me about their money. If they can't, I can't do my job. But you can't figure out personality from a CV. You have to discover that yourself.

You should be asking:

- Will this person fit in with the culture of the company?
- Will I like working with them?
- Will we be able to work through problems together?
- How do they attack problems?
- What kind of mindset do they have?

Experience and skills will get the right people through the gate, but I advise you to make your final decision based on chemistry and personality fit. Don't waste time hiring someone who's qualified but impossible to work with. What a waste of time and money. Find someone you can trust to take care of their operational role and your money. If you can't trust the people you work with, what's the point? If you can only work with them when business is good but not when business is bad, why are they there?

Can't I Just Hire a Friend?

I know it's difficult to hire a stranger to manage your money, but don't use trust as an excuse to hire your best friend or partner just because it's easier. You need staff who can stay objective, who are qualified and experienced. If you must work with a partner or friend, make sure you put them in an appropriate role for their qualifications and skills. Do not hire your partner to help with bookkeeping if they're not a qualified accountant. I've seen that too many times in companies I've worked in, and it's just too risky: there will be gaps in their knowledge that could cost you money. That returns us to my original argument: hire someone you could trust. A good hire could end up becoming a friend, anyway.

What if the Needs of My Business Change?

What you need when you're doing £200k of revenue is not the same as you need when you're doing £20 million of revenue. The roles and people you hire will change. If you hire someone who's right for a role, and that role changes, change the person, too. If you don't want to rehire because you like the person, move them to a different position in the business. Don't keep the wrong people in the wrong roles just because you're friends. That person will either get overwhelmed, mess up, or quit, and things between you will get awkward. People respond much better if they understand why a decision has been made and are kept informed, so communicate why things are changing. If you've hired based on a good chemistry fit and trust, moving your staff around shouldn't be that hard.

Minimal Input, Maximum Output

I always come back to the word 'efficiency'. How can we be more efficient with our money and our work? How can we improve our cashflow or our bottom line (profit)? Business is about tweaking the resources you have, money and time, to help you get to your goal. That Magic Number. If you are bootstrapping your business or working on two hours of sleep every day, finding out that you're bleeding money or wasting time will really demotivate you. You need people to help you.

When we've worked so hard to start a business, it can be difficult to trust and let go of the controls. But at some point, you either have to accept that you're going to hit a ceiling alone, or you've got to invite other people in to help you. We always need help to grow and scale, and hiring someone to take care of operations is a smart, tried-and-tested way to get you there. If you think you need operational help but you're not sure where to start, just be curious. Is there someone out there who does this for a living? Does this job exist? Does anyone know someone who does something similar? Wellbeing officers, data scientists and content creators didn't exist thirty years ago, but those new roles were invented to meet the needs of businesses today. If you need someone to help you and the role doesn't exist, create it and then hire for it. It is your business. Make it work for you.

Case Study: Lifestyle Business – School Run Studio

Michelle and James had a friend doing their bookkeeping, but she wasn't qualified. They had an end-of-year accountant to whom they sent a bunch of spreadsheets and receipts. Nothing wrong with that, but they couldn't get the strategic financial advice they needed, and it was a very old-fashioned way of working. When School Run Studio hired me as their Finance Manager, I was able to modernise and streamline everything for them. I set them up with a cloud-based accounting package and showed them how to log the data themselves. As it was just the two of them with a very small Lifestyle business, there was no need for anything more complex. Then, I worked with them on the strategy side to find business trends, ensure they were getting a good ROI on outgoings and help them become more efficient. They didn't need me in a full-time role, just once a week, every quarter, and that was enough to transform their business.

Case Study: Legacy Business – Evergreen Assembly

They had previously outsourced their financial functions so didn't have anyone doing finance from within. That can be a really good way to start when you're small because you can take advantage of a large pool of outsourced accountants to manage payroll, accounts receivable and all of that. The drawback is that you're just a client, a number on a spreadsheet. You don't necessarily get the responsiveness or the personal attention that you would get from someone working within your business. Also, Evergreen Assembly had reached a point where they were too big for an outsourced function. It was actually the outsourced company that approached me and said, "This is too big for us. Can you help them take it in-house?"

I went in thinking that I was going to bring everything in-house and lead the strategy side of things, with someone else to do all the bookkeeping. But that's not what happened. Evergreen Assembly thought they wanted someone to help with the financial strategy and the growth of the business, but what they really wanted was someone to execute the decisions they made. They were excited about the experience I would bring but didn't expect me to be as vocal about strategy and business as I was. As with all Legacy businesses, when the goal isn't profit and the mission is personal, it can cloud your judgement. You ignore advice that could grow your business, so be self-aware. What do you really want with this hire? You don't have to agree with everything your hire says, but don't get someone to help you and then ignore their advice. This is why it's really important to get the right person for the right role.

Case Study: Business to Sell – Brass Tacks Collective

Brass Tacks Collective's finances were outsourced, with Hannah doing a lot in-house, too. However, she was too stretched, so I was brought in to help take the burden off her. But I don't think they had realised they could bring a financial expert in who could add value to the strategy and growth of the company. Very quickly, they saw what a CFO could offer, and I was soon involved in most of the business decisions. However, a mistake I made was trying to do everything myself and not having an assistant to help with my operations. The work nearly killed me. I worked ninety hours a week for a year. I should have taken my own advice and hired someone to help me, and because of that, I was grossly underpaid. But that was my own fault. I should have said, "No. This is too much for one person."

If you hire someone, make sure you know what they can bring to your business, and use all the skills they have to offer. Listen to them if they say they can do more and give them support if they need it. If Simon and Hannah had kept me in my original role and ignored the advice I could offer, they never would have realised that the US held more money for them, and they wouldn't have walked away with millions when they exited.

Think Like a CFO

Consider the key financial responsibilities you'd like help with in your business right now:

- What financial knowledge do you wish you had?
- Do you want someone to just do the books, or do you want strategic help?
- Do you need to outsource anything?

Check the table/reference guide on the next page. Write down three roles from the guide you would like to have (or have in the future) in your business. What value could they add? Then rank them in order of importance.

RESOURCE

MENU OF FINANCIAL ROLES A.K.A. THE MATRIX OF NERDS

Use this to start thinking about who you need to hire now. Do you want them on a fractional contract or full-time? Who will you need in three to five years?

*CFO is an American term that has gained popularity in the UK, but it's just another word for Finance Director. The terms are interchangeable but mean the same.

Bookkeeper

Topline Responsibilities & Business Influence

Records financial transactions, manages ledgers, and reconciles bank statements

Not Responsible For

Financial forecasting, tax planning, and high-level financial reporting

Business Size Suitability

Small businesses, freelancers, and startups

Business Support

Responsible for record-keeping, not strategic decisions

Accounts Payable Clerk

Topline Responsibilities & Business Influence

Processes payments to suppliers, manages invoices, and ensures bills are paid on time

Not Responsible For

Budgeting, financial forecasting, and tax compliance

Business Size Suitability

SMEs, large businesses, and enterprises

Business Support

Ensures financial accuracy but no strategic input

Accounts Receivable Clerk

Topline Responsibilities & Business Influence

Manages incoming payments, invoices clients, and follows up on overdue payments

Not Responsible For

Financial strategy, tax planning, and budgeting

Business Size Suitability

SMEs, large businesses, and enterprises

Business Support

Responsible for record-keeping. Supports cash flow but has no role in decision making

Financial Controller

Topline Responsibilities & Business Influence

Oversees financial reporting, budgeting, and internal controls

Not Responsible For

Auditing, external financial compliance (handled by auditors)

Business Size Suitability

SMEs, large businesses, and multinational corporations

Business Support

Oversees financial reporting, budgeting, and controls. Some business influence and are responsible for financial decision-making

Chief Financial Officer (CFO)

Topline Responsibilities & Business Influence

Leads financial strategy, risk management, financial planning, and investor relations

Not Responsible For

Day-to-day bookkeeping, processing payments

Business Size Suitability

Large businesses, multinational corporations

Business Support

Leads financial strategy and planning; key influential role in decision-making and business growth. High business influence and is responsible for strategic decisions

Auditor

Topline Responsibilities & Business Influence

Examines financial statements for accuracy and compliance, conducts risk assessments

Not Responsible For

Daily financial management, budgeting, and financial strategy

Business Size Suitability

SMEs, large businesses, and multinational corporations

Business Support

Moderate business support but not involved in strategy

Management Accountant

Topline Responsibilities & Business Influence

Prepares financial reports for internal decision-making, cost analysis, and budgeting. Moderate business influence

Not Responsible For

External financial reporting, tax compliance

Business Size Suitability

SMEs, large businesses, and multinational corporations

Business Support

Responsible for record-keeping and some strategic input. Provides financial reports and budgeting insights; supports internal decision-making with moderate influence

Tax Accountant

Topline Responsibilities & Business Influence

Manages tax compliance, prepares tax returns, and ensures adherence to tax laws. Responsible for tax strategy but not broader financial strategy

Not Responsible For

General bookkeeping, financial forecasting, business strategy

Business Size Suitability

Freelancers, SMEs, large businesses, and multinational corporations

Business Support

Manages tax compliance and strategy; supports financial efficiency but not broader business strategy

Financial Analyst

Topline Responsibilities & Business Influence

Analyses financial data, prepares reports for decision-making, and supports investment planning

Not Responsible For

Daily bookkeeping, tax compliance

Business Size Suitability

SMEs, large businesses, multinational corportions

Business Support

Analyses financial data for insights; supports investment and business strategy and can contribute to strategic decisions

Payroll Specialist

Topline Responsibilities & Business Influence

Processes employee salaries, tax deductions, and ensures payroll compliance

Not Responsible For

Financial strategy, investment planning

Business Size Suitability

SMEs, large businesses, and multinational corporations

Business Support

Processes salaries and ensures payroll compliance; essential for record-keeping and employee compensation but not strategic

Forensic Accountant

Topline Responsibilities & Business Influence

Investigates financial fraud, analyses discrepancies, and provides litigation support. Responsible for financial investigations but not day-to-day finance operations. Moderate business influence

Not Responsible For

Budgeting, payroll, cash flow management

Business Size Suitability

Large businesses, multinational corporations

Business Support

Investigates financial discrepancies and fraud; moderate business support with legal implications

Investment Analyst

Topline Responsibilities & Business Influence

Evaluates investment opportunities, advises on financial portfolios

Not Responsible For

Tax compliance, payroll management

Business Size Suitability

Large businesses, multinational corporations

Business Support

Evaluates and advises on investments; supports financial growth, but not general business operations. Some business influence and responsible for investment decisions

12

F*CK THE PING PONG TABLE –
WHERE'S THE BONUS?

— Incentives —

Think about the people you work with now or could work with in the future.

Who are they?
What are they like?
What do they bring to your company?

If you've taken my advice on hiring, they're probably bloody brilliant people you could not live without who are absolutely transformative to the business: they are the marketing director who spotted a trend and jumped on it in time, doubling your revenue; or your VA who streamlined all your systems so now you have ten extra hours in your week. While you might have done most of the work at the beginning of your entrepreneurial journey, you have met and hired people, loyal counterparts and partners who have changed it in ways you couldn't have done on your own.

It is only fair that you show those essential people that they are valued. The last thing you want is for one of the most intelligent, talented people you've ever hired to leave and take all that potential with them.

So, once you find good people, keep them.

(Don't) Pay Them With Pizza

The more you take people on the journey with you and reward them for it, the more they will give you and your business in return. But don't assume that free breakfasts or a pool table are the solution to keeping good people. Pizza Fridays and your dry cleaning paid for are perks. Private medical insurance, pensions and an extra day of holiday are benefits. All lovely things that can add tangible value to an employee's workday, but they won't stop a key member of staff from leaving if they're underpaid or poorly treated.

You need to give them a piece of the pie: share the rewards they have helped to build. Give them an incentive.

Incentives: Fixed/Retention Bonuses

The most familiar incentive you might have heard of is a fixed/retention bonus. It is a financial reward tied to some fixed time period or the sale of the business. This can be done on top of annual bonuses and commissions.

Examples are:

- A time-dependent bonus, like an annual bonus or staying for a fixed number of years.
- If the company sells, the employee who has stayed for an agreed time gets a bonus.
- A long-term investment plan (LTIP).

Incentives: Shares

The other type is offering shares. More people are recognising that wealth comes from owning assets that bring in revenue rather than exchanging time for money. It is no secret that owning property has always been a popular wealth-building asset. But now it is becoming normalised to build businesses and side hustles, too. In the UK, over 900,000 businesses were incorporated in 2023,[27] up 12% from the previous year. Online courses, apps and platforms now educate people about cryptocurrency, the stock market, or how to buy and sell collectables. 'Passive income' is a buzzword. People want a piece of the pie. If you want the best people in your business, you've got to give them an asset: shares. If I'm working with someone and I own a percentage of that business, I will put way more effort into it than if I'm just paid every month.

Most companies have one type of share that gives you and investors voting rights and profits. But as the director of a limited company, you can create other types of shares, or 'share classes', which give different rights. These are usually called alphabet shares (A-class shares, B-class shares and so on). For example, B-class shareholders can have rights to dividends but not voting rights. C-class shareholders might only have the right to profits after a company has been sold. There are loads of ways of divvying up your company, and you can choose how to do it, but as long as you retain 50% or more of the company, you retain control. This is just about rewarding people for their work, loyalty and commitment, which, when you're trying to build, is a good thing.

There are other share structures you can use, like:

- An Employee Ownership Trust: a trust that holds shares of a company on behalf of the employees.
- EMI Schemes: an HMRC initiative that gives employees share options that have tax benefits if the company ever sells.
- Growth shares: a share that is only valuable after someone has joined and has helped to grow the value of a company to an agreed valuation.

There is a lot of flexibility in the types of incentives you can offer, so find one that works with your business but is also attractive to your staff. There is no minimum business size for offering share schemes, and in some ways it's better to set up the scheme earlier as the share value grows with the business. Tracking that growth can be motivating for the employees. Alternatively, if you're still small and growing, you can offer a promise of shares or shares when certain KPIs are reached, like doing x number of years in service. You can also simply link a financial reward to an event, so you do not part with any cash unless, and until, that event happens, i.e. if the company sells, you get £200k.

Rules of Incentives

From 2019 to 2021, I worked with a tech firm where every single person, regardless of their role, was part of the company's EMI scheme. I have never seen a company with staff so driven. It was phenomenal. None of them was particularly highly paid, but they all understood the journey they were on together, and they were all so motivated that they worked their backsides off. They were buzzed and fired up for it because they knew what was expected of them and what the plan was. Any incentive you offer must be realistic, measurable and achievable for you and your staff. It is also a good idea to do it earlier rather than later, as the more growth employees get to share in, the more motivated they are.

Whatever you offer, you have to see it through. Otherwise, it's not an incentive. Employees need to pay their bills, so don't offer them an incentive that has no hope of ever materialising. That is just a lottery ticket in disguise. It is a piece of paper that may, or may not, pay out. An incentive scheme is not an underhanded way to keep people in your team while paying them less than they're worth. People will see through it, and that won't retain or motivate anyone. Provide clear guidelines about what's expected of your staff and what's in it for them, and help them decide if it's worth staying for.

No One Likes Mouldy Pic

Okay, so this is a financial literacy book, so I obviously have to remind you that if you're going to give incentives, you have to make sure the finances work. All schemes carry different tax impacts; therefore, it's always sensible to take advice when planning what incentives you want to offer.

Do not offer people shares or LTIPs if your company isn't making a profit: that's offering people shares of nothing – and that is just taking the piss. If you promise your staff bonuses or shares, you have to be able to afford it, so put a little provision in every month, and make it part of your cash flow forecast and budget. You can't make promises like that and then not come through on them. It is wonderful to give people a piece of the pie, but if you're putting a piece away in a little box that no one has any hope of eating, it'll just go mouldy. And no one wants mouldy pie.

The Bullshit 'Self-Made Millionaire'

In my opinion, businesses that underperform are ones that view people as assets and resources rather than individuals who can shape the success of a business. That is why I don't believe anyone who says they did it all themselves. Absolute bullshit. They might sit there and say they did it on their own, but they didn't. They had help, whether it was tangible or not. Good people are essential, not expendable. If someone quits, you can't just replace them with someone of equal expertise and experience. Impossible. No two accountants, salespeople or managers are the same, and they will all bring something different to your journey. Maybe you could do it without those special few people, but it might be a far less lucrative and pleasant journey if you tried. Growing a business can be lonely, and you'll only realise how valuable people like that are when they're gone and the gap they leave is too big to ignore. That is why it is right to have a slightly smaller piece of a bigger pie and share it with people who have massively added to it, not just from a moral perspective but from a growth perspective. When people feel valued and recognised, they are more likely to return the favour. And that can only do good things for your bottom line.

Think Like a CFO

You can create any bonus you want as long as you are not asking someone to sell you their soul. As long as it has some tangible value for both you and your employee, and you have the legal paperwork to record the agreement, you can offer whatever you want. So start thinking about what kind of incentives you would like to offer.

- Do your staff (or future staff) like the idea of owning a percentage of a business?
- Or would a fixed sum after a period of time be more attractive?
- Would you like it to be tied to an event?
- Does opening a trust or scheme sound good?

13

SHOW ME THE MONEY

— *Funding* —

I once knew an incredibly talented entrepreneur, a creative, who had been nominated for numerous awards and even won an entrepreneurial grant for her work. However, she struggled to get investment. Any support she did manage to secure was a bad fit or took advantage of her business to the point that she started to believe her work wasn't viable. She believed so much in the actual products and you could see the passion in her work. However, the business side was killing her: she desperately needed funding to scale. But she was starting to think it would never happen.

In the UK, female entrepreneurs are less likely to scale up to £1 million turnover than men. 29% of male entrepreneurs, once their business is established, eventually achieve the £1–50 million turnover mark. But only 13%[28] of women running established businesses do the same.

That needs to change.

How you want to grow your business is entirely your choice; you don't have to scale to millions in revenue if you don't want to. Not every person has to aim for the moon, so if you don't want to work with an investor, don't. It is not all rainbows and sunshine. But you should always know your options. Knowledge is power, after all. No business owner is required to take on funding or investment, but if you do, it could be the difference between having a side hustle and having a business that gives you all the financial freedom you've ever dreamed of.

Why Bother With Funding?

I once got chatting with the owner of a MedTech company. They had designed a piece of medical tech to test the effects of an anaesthetic while in a patient's bloodstream. It was very clever. But there was still a long way to go.

"We've built prototypes and we know hospitals need this," they explained once we got talking, "but..." and they screwed up their face like they'd smelled something bad, "We need funding to put testing in place. We need case studies to show it works and the impact it can have."

"Have you applied for any government grants?" I asked. They replied that they had applied for several, but they took years to get... years they didn't have.

They needed funding. They had investors in mind who were interested, but they knew it needed the backup of financial evidence if they wanted to be taken seriously. With my help, they could build solid financial models of what they needed and credibly demonstrate how it would be used. In comparison, someone running a marketing or recruitment business or a small independent shop would probably manage on their own. They could take funding if they wanted, but it wouldn't be as essential.

Having an extra boost of cash, whether it's £5k or £5 million, will always help you grow faster. But the experience of working with an investor or being indebted to a bank could be an absolute pain in the ass, depending on how you go about it. That is why it's important to decide whether you'd get funding even before you ever need it.

When Should I Get It?

All companies reach a point at which their growth becomes difficult, where, without significant funding, it'll take so long that it's not worth the effort. Unless you're in a very fast-moving industry or you're in the research and development side of science, where you need funding quickly and up front, you should usually wait until you feel that squeeze and you start to notice that it is getting to be bloody hard work. You notice you could do with an extra £500 here, or you need £3k for that. You need to hire another person, or you need equipment you can't afford. You start to think, "If I just had a bit more money, I could do that."

I don't want to understate how much hard work it is to grow a business, but overall, getting to a million pounds in revenue is fairly easy. But going from a million to £5 million is hard work. Really hard work. Once you get through that, you can probably go as far as you want. But it's that squeeze that's the challenge.

Which Type of Funding Should I Get?

There are two types of funding you can use:

> **Debt** → someone loans you money.

> **Equity** → you give up a share of your business in exchange for money.

Equity

If you are happy with the idea of giving away shares in return for funding, there are pros and cons to think about.

Pros:

- An equity shareholder will either be an individual or a private company that is well-connected in the industry you're trying to enter.

- You are more likely to grow faster than if you did it alone because your investor will be motivated to make their money back.
- You will benefit from connections, knowledge and partnerships they have that could help grow your business.
- You share the risk and stress of growing a business with someone who's done it before.

Cons:

- You are giving away part of your company, which could mean giving away voting rights or creative control, depending on what you've agreed to.
- If you give away a large percentage of equity in your company, say 40%, they own that much of your assets and profit. If you make £1 million in profit, they are entitled to £400,000 of that.
- If you partner with an investor you have a bad relationship with, you have no choice but to keep working with them until they sell their shares or you buy them out.
- If they think your business is a risky investment, they could ask for more equity as a way to minimise their risk, meaning less of the pie for you.

Equity Crowdfunding

This is a slightly different type of equity funding, where you list your company on an online platform so investors and members of the public can buy shares in your business. Each platform has its own rules about how the process is done. Your challenge is to offer something exciting for the public. If BrewDog were to crowdfund, they'd make a fortune. If I were to crowdfund, nobody would give a crap. It has to be something the average person wants to put their money into. Always do your research before you go down this path.

Debt

If you don't like the idea of giving a share of your company away, debt is a good alternative: a loan or overdraft from a bank or building society. However, we all have negative associations with the word 'debt', and if your brain doesn't like 'debt' hanging over your head, it can be quite stressful. The bank's repayments always come before your own, and you have to pay it back regardless of whether you've made any profit or not.

Pros:

- You don't have to give away equity or control.
- You don't have to get into a business partnership with someone you might not work well with.
- No one owns your assets or profit but you.

Cons:

- Banks only give loans to businesses that fulfil specific criteria.
- They don't care about your mission or what change you could create in the world.
- They look at how strong your balance sheet is and how well you've managed your money so far. If you're still finding your way and making mistakes, they won't help you.
- If you don't make your repayments, the bank could take your assets or close your business.
- If you take out a payday loan, or you make a decision under stress, you could end up paying disgusting interest rates.

Other Sources

Invoice Funding

This is where a bank loans you a percentage of the money you're invoicing. When the invoice gets paid by your client, you pay the bank back – with interest. Banks only do this in certain circumstances, but it can be really useful if you're a massive project-based business and you're struggling with cash flow because you're new.

Grants

There are tons of government and industry grants around. But they are, as you would imagine, an absolute pain in the ass to get. You generally have to be doing something different or new with your business. And they take months to come to a decision, by which time you might be past the point of needing the bloody money anyway. Grants are like a cherry on the cake. They are useful but shouldn't be your main source of investment.

Tax Relief

R&D tax funding is a tax credit offered by HMRC. It is not funding in the same way as other types, but it can help reduce your corporate tax bill if you're involved in some sort of research and development. There are many ways to get tax relief or tax allowances, but you need to speak to a tax advisor.

Decide whether to choose debt or equity *before* you look into funding. If the life of your business depends on this decision, you're already in a dangerous position. You are too vulnerable financially and emotionally, and you risk making a reactive decision. This means you risk giving away too much of your business in exchange for equity, or agreeing to crappy loan rates. Decide on your preference before you start. What are you comfortable with, and what are you not?

Do I Really Need to Make Millions?

No, you don't. But if you have dreams of living in a world with better healthcare, better education and better opportunities for young girls and boys, you might want to think about aiming high. Because when women have financial power, *everyone* sees the benefits. You might think that in order to become wealthy, you have to become some sort of Scrooge, wealthy but mean and cold-hearted, loved by no one. But that is far from the truth. Female entrepreneurs are more likely to create businesses that have a positive social impact. We are more likely to create or invest in businesses that support ESG[29] issues (Environmental, Social and Governance). Even when women do become massively wealthy, they still use it to impact society positively:

Melanie Perkins[30] is the CEO and co-founder of Canva and has a net worth of $3.6 billion. With her husband, they set up the Canva Foundation, pledging to commit their 30% equity in the company to philanthropy. At the time of writing, they've donated $14 million to charities.

Ruth Gottesman, widow of Berkshire Hathaway investor David Gottesman, donated $1 billion in 2024 to cover tuition fees for medical students at Albert Einstein College of Medicine, where she used to work as a professor. She inherited the money when David died in September 2022 and was left with the whole portfolio of Berkshire Hathaway stock. His instructions were that she 'do whatever [she] thinks is right with it."[31]

Taylor Swift donated to food banks[32] in the UK and internationally during her Eras Tour in 2023 and regularly donates to disaster relief funds such as those for the LA Wildfires in 2025, hurricane relief in 2024 and tornado relief funds in 2023.[33]

Women can and do make a difference with money. So, if your goal is to earn millions and change the world, do it.

Think Like A CFO

Think about the three ways you can grow your business:

- Organic (bootstrapped)
- Equity Funded
- Debt Funded

Write your own pros and cons list for these options to clarify your comfort levels for each.

Now, think about your business's current growth goals: how could they be best served? Via organic growth or an injection of cash from external funding?

Then, say you were to magically receive external funding, how much quicker do you think you would reach your goal?

Re-read your pros and cons for that type of funding and see if your thoughts have changed.

14

FUCK POLITENESS, ASK FOR WHAT YOU WANT

— Investors —

Picking an investor is like getting into bed with someone you don't know. It could be amazing, could be shit. Who knows? You are committing to someone you know very little about, taking their money and giving them part of your company in return. You don't know how things will work out. So you have to be careful. If they're charming and tick all the boxes, but you feel railroaded into uncomfortable situations, or they don't listen, is that really worth the stress for the next five to ten years? Of course, you could absolutely smash your numbers and have the best idea, but if *you're* an arrogant ass, they won't want to work with you, either. It is still a business of people and relationships: find the right match.

There are two main types of investors you will meet when you start and grow a business:

Angel Investors

These are rich or high-net-worth individuals who invest their own money into a company, usually at the early stage known as the 'pre-seed' stage. They are more likely to be people who have philanthropic goals, who want to pass on their knowledge, or who have sold a business and want to help other small businesses. As well as capital, they can offer mentorship and guidance. This is good for businesses still in the market research or concept stage, where the risk is still quite high. Their investment will generally be small, and you might work together for a few years.

VCs (Venture Capitalists)

When you're ready to scale up, venture capitalists can take you to the next level. They have access to a pooled source of money, often made up of pension funds, other institutions and rich individuals. They will make much larger investments than angel investors and will expect more control over business decisions, but they will have teams and niche expertise that can help you. They will prefer businesses that already have a good track record or definite growth potential.

There are a few other types you need to know about, such as Private Equity firms, banks, and peer-to-peer lenders (friends/ acquaintances), but you don't need to worry about them until you're an established business with proven success. But start researching them now and meeting people who work in them. They could be helpful to you in the future.

What Will Investors Look For?

All investors, no matter what their background, gender or race, will prefer to invest in industries or products they have experience of and understand. You are not likely to get an investment in a new drug from someone experienced in retail; they wouldn't have a clue. An investor's goal is to make money, ultimately. They won't partner with someone if they don't think they'll make a profit.

For most people, the only time they'll ever see an investor is on the TV show *Dragons' Den*, a show so hyped up and dramatised that you don't get the true picture. But it is good at demonstrating that you can be spectacularly good at what you do, and you could have an amazing product or service, but if you don't know your numbers and you can't answer their questions, you won't get any money. They want low risk with high return, which means they want a business owner who knows how to manage their money: a company with a proven track record of not wasting cash and with the potential for growth and healthy profits. With so much at risk, it's exactly why investors are famous for asking difficult questions. You need to be able to defend all your business decisions, the good ones and the bad, and prove that you can run your business in a responsible way. No founder will have a perfect understanding of their numbers, and investors are aware of this, but if you can go in there with confidence, you are more likely to win them over.

What Should I Do to Start?

Your balance sheet, cash flow and P&L will tell investors what they need to know about your business. But you will still be questioned hard about them. So make sure you understand what kind of picture they tell:

- **If your P&L shows a steady and consistent growth in profit** → You know how to grow a business strategically and carefully.
- **If you have minimal ups and downs** → You can spread the risk and are in control of your revenue and costs. It suggests good client management and anticipation of problems.
- **Spikes and dips that can be explained** → A spike or dip in profits that can be explained with a valid reason suggests good planning, e.g. your supplier was having a massive sale, so you bought three months' worth of stock instead of one.
- **You have more assets than liabilities** → A positive balance sheet will tell them that your business is resilient.
- **A cash reserve** → You are prepared for unexpected costs.

If your numbers don't say anything positive, wait and get your numbers in order. If that means waiting a few years before meeting with investors, that's perfectly fine. Don't manipulate your numbers to make you look better than you are. Instead, work on improving the consistency of your profit line, get rid of a few liabilities and build up your cash reserve. Investors will do their due diligence, so don't give them any reason to say no. Give them a good few years of solid numbers to prove you're not a liability.

✎ Investors look at a huge number of ratios to determine how resilient, and therefore potentially profitable, your business is. If you're curious about which ratios they could ask you about, I've put a list of them at the end of this chapter. There is also a short overview of pitch decks below if you are curious about pitching to investors.

What if I Get Nervous?

All founders get nervous, no matter what their background, gender or experience. You are in a vulnerable position because you're asking a very powerful person to take a chance on you and your business. It is a big deal. So you have to prepare. Your numbers will reveal everything, and they will be looking for reasons *not* to invest. So, know and understand how your numbers got where they are and what the forecast for your business is. If that means practising your pitch beforehand, getting a communication or speech coach or just doing some roleplays, do it. Like a good speech or TEDx talk, you have to captivate them with a good story. (This is probably why *Dragons' Den* is so popular.) However, even the best stories won't matter if you're easily thrown off by a difficult question. Investors will come at you with complete scepticism. That means they will ask difficult questions that could put you in a flap and make you fumble. Your numbers could be amazing, but if you can't control your fears, none of that will matter.

Nobody's Perfect

The investors you meet will probably have built and lost fifty businesses, and they will have made mistakes too. If they question an anomaly in your data or a decision you're not proud of, it's okay to be honest and say what went wrong. Calmly explain why it happened and what measures you've put in place to make sure it doesn't happen again. Show them you're low-risk, high-reward.

Take cash flow. Say they notice your clients aren't paying you quickly enough, which makes them think, "Hmm, crap credit control." If you tell them you've now hired someone dedicated purely to credit control, and you get quarterly reports, that tells them you've learned and fixed the problem. Anything in your financials that sticks out as unusual or problematic will be analysed, so have decent responses prepared.

Just try it. How would you respond to these questions?

- Why did you lose three members of staff?
- Why do you have a spike in your profits in March?
- Why did you buy that asset? It doesn't seem like it adds value.
- What is this liability for?
- Why is your rent 15% of your revenue?

Be ready for everything and always show them you know how to minimise risk:

- "We are working towards making sure that no client is worth more than 20% of our revenue. And here are the stats to show you where we're at."
- "I've engaged with an HR consultant who now does six-monthly reviews of the market to see what salaries we should be paying everyone. And we have a provision for pay increases should we determine that someone has been underpaid for a period."
- "We took on too many clients in January, which put a huge amount of pressure on our delivery team, and we didn't have the opportunity to hire additional resources. That has artificially inflated our profits, and we now have a bank of temporary resources to lean on should client demand spike."

With Great Power Comes Great Responsibility

There is credibility and power that will come from having an investment. It demonstrates that you can manage your money, you know your numbers, and you can give a return on investment: your ideas and knowledge matter. From the bigger picture, all the way down to the granular stuff, you can handle it.

This is a historically male-dominated industry, and with 58%[34] of venture capitalists being white males and only 2% of investment going to female founders, you have to be aware of what you're walking into. That is not to say they won't invest, and many VC firms have quotas that support female-led companies. However, "Founders unfortunately still get more attention when they are focused on subjects that male investors can connect to," according to Juliette Mauro,[35] co-founder of Femtech France. So, you need to create an airtight case for why your business is worth investing in. Blow them away with your numbers and your ideas, and show them how smart they would be to invest in you and your business.

Think Like a CFO

Have a look at your numbers now if you have them.

- If you were an investor, what would make you ask questions?
- Do you have anomalies and unexplained numbers?
- What can you do to fix them?
- How would you respond if an investor questioned them in a meeting?

Guide to Pitch Decks

I am not an expert in pitch decks, but I have worked alongside owners who have gone through the process, so here are a few key things you need to think about and prepare before you build your deck.

Design

Pitch decks are an art. You are trying to prove why it has to be you and why it has to be now, so they require some creativity. As well as telling a great story and giving a good performance, your deck has to be just as powerful. Include beautiful visuals and eye-catching design. If you go to a restaurant that serves delicious food but the waiters are surly, the wallpaper's peeling and the food arrives looking like a dog's dinner, you probably won't put it in your mouth and discover how delicious it is. Investors use their gut and their emotions. If they don't like what they're looking at before you've even told them anything about it, you're done before you open your mouth.

Size

No more than fifteen slides: nobody pays attention for any longer. If you haven't won them over in that many slides, another five won't make a difference!

Problem

Describe the ideal customer and the problem(s) they face. Give detailed information on their demographics, their pain points, how the problem impacts them, and why it needs to be fixed. Provide evidence of why these people are impacted by the problem you solve. You need to demonstrate that you know this customer inside and out. Why is it a problem worth solving?

Solution

What is the ideal outcome for your customer, and how is your solution unique? There needs to be a big outcome – a significant change or impact on the customer that has a sense of urgency to it. There needs to be a quantifiable outcome, too. Not just 'they'll be less tired'. You have to show that the problem needs to be solved now, and it's best solved by you.

Business Model

Provide calculations that go right back to the moment money changes hands, i.e. the moment the product or service is sold. How have you arrived at the projections of selling to one thousand customers per month at £20 per customer? Be specific. Show how you have reached those numbers, otherwise, they'll think you've just plucked them from your backside. Don't type hard-coded numbers in; every number should link to another, right down to the individual sale and every cost that goes along with it. It needs to be realistic, and you need to be able to defend every number you've used. This is where knowing your numbers comes in, as investors are looking for evidence that you know your market and customers deeply. You also need to show the investor how much money they'll get back and when. Models need to be flexible, i.e. be able to respond to smaller/greater uptake than you've anticipated.

Market

Don't just launch into a 'this is a billion-dollar market' sales pitch. Start by showing the market you've already captured, how you've captured it, and how much your customers are already paying to solve this problem. Then build up to how many people you're going to capture, how many people other companies are capturing and how you're going to get to those levels. Just talk about your niche, not the entire market.

Competition

Who are they, where are they, what are they doing, how are they solving this problem, and why is your solution better? How much of the market do they currently have, and how have they captured it? How long have they been in the market, why does the market still exist, and how will you stop them from coming up with the same solution as you? Show them you're aware of the challenges your business faces.

Team

Who are your fellow saviours? Why are they on the journey with you and what do they bring with them? Why shouldn't the investor just hire your team and build this themselves? How will you retain the team?

Traction

Is this the right time to invest? Is it too early or too late? There needs to be demonstrable traction or momentum building in your market, something that creates an urgency to solve the problem you want to solve. You also need to show that the solution you bring is what the customer actually wants. That could be via research or results, but it needs to be from the customer's perspective, not just you telling the customer about the product/service and asking what they think of your solution and then expecting the investor to buy into it. Don't forget, the investor probably isn't facing the problem you're trying to sell, so they need to understand it and buy into it.

Investment

How much money are you asking for? Be _very_ specific about how you will use it. It is not just 'marketing' or 'working capital'. How long will it take? How much is being spent? Where and what results will it yield? KPIs are critical here to demonstrate a measurable outcome that can't be achieved without the investment.

You

Position yourself as the saviour. Remember, this is all about them believing that you are the one to solve this problem: you know your sh*t. Bring the investor in and make them see you as a worthy saviour before you tell them what you're going to save. They need to buy into you before they buy into what you're selling. Make it personal and show some personality.

A massive amount of detail and thought needs to go into a deck, so I recommend finding a professional who specialises in creating pitch decks for investment meetings. Your potential investor needs to buy into you as a person as well as the product or service you're selling. So, do everything you can to present yourself in the best light. Make them feel that not investing would be a mistake.

Metrics that Investors might ask you about

Gross Margin %	
Why it Matters	**Formula**
How much profit does this company make after paying its cost of goods sold?	Gross profit ÷ Revenue x 100

Operating Margin %	
Why it Matters	**Formula**
What is the operating efficiency of a company? How much of its revenue turns into profit?	Operating profit(before tax) ÷ Revenue x 100

Return on Assets	
Why it Matters	**Formula**
How efficiently does this company use its assets to generate profit?	Net profit (after tax) ÷ Total assets

Return on Equity	
Why it Matters	**Formula**
How efficiently does this company use its equity to generate profit?	Net profit (after tax) ÷ Shareholder's equity

Current Ratio	
Why it Matters	**Formula**
What is this company's ability to pay off short-term liabilities with current assets?	Current assets ÷ Current liabilities

Acid-Test Ratio	
Why it Matters	**Formula**
What is this company's ability to pay off short-term liabilities with near-cash assets?	Current assets - Inventories) ÷ Current liabilities

Cash Ratio

Why it Matters	Formula
What is this company's ability to pay off short-term liabilities with cash and cash equivalents?	Cash and Cash Equivalents ÷ Current Liabilities

Operating Cash Flow Ratio

Why it Matters	Formula
How many times can this company can pay off current liabilities with the cash generated in a given period?	Cash flow from Operations ÷ Current liabilities

Debt to Asset Ratio

Why it Matters	Formula
Measures how many of your assets have been funded by debt	Total liabilities ÷ Total assets

Debt to Equity Ratio

Why it Matters	Formula
What is the burden of total debt and financial liabilities against shareholders' equity?	Total liabilities ÷ Shareholder's equity

Interest Coverage Ratio

Why it Matters	Formula
How easily can this company pay its interest expenses on borrowings?	EBIT ÷ Interest expenses

Asset Turnover Ratio

Why it Matters	Formula
What is this company's ability to generate revenue from its assets?	Revenue ÷ Average total assets

Inventory Turnover Ratio	
Why it Matters	Formula
How many times is this company's inventory sold and replaced over a given period?	Cost of goods sold ÷ Average inventory

Cash Flow Coverage Ratio	
Why it Matters	Formula
Does this company have cash flow to pay for scheduled debt (including interest) payments on its debt?	Operating cash flows ÷ Total debt

Cash Flow Margin Ratio	
Why it Matters	Formula
How much cash is generated per pound of revenue? (Offers a clearer picture than net profit.)	Cash flow from operations ÷ Revenue

Current Liability Coverage Ratio	
Why it Matters	Formula
Can this business generate enough cash to pay for its immediate obligations?	Cash flow from operations ÷ Average current liabilities

MINI-CHAPTER: NEED TO KNOW

WHY MORE WOMEN SHOULD BECOME INVESTORS

The investment world is still heavily male-dominated. Only 15% of venture capitalist 'cheque-writers'[36] (investors who make the funding decision) are women, and globally only 10%[37] of senior positions in private equity and venture capital firms are women.

That is a problem. If money only flows through the same people who make the same decisions, hold the same ideas and share the same values, it ends up going to the same places. This leaves certain markets overlooked and underserved because the innovation and money they need never appear.

While there are women who work in investment and have the power to make those decisions, it's not enough. The majority tend to be found in more junior or operational roles, with fewer women being promoted or retained for leadership positions the higher you go up the ladder.[38][39]

We need more female investors to rise to the top. We have to step into these roles. We have to become more visible, become more willing to take risks and more willing to fuck it up.

Women are shown to be better leaders,[40] so it stands to reason they will be better founders, produce better returns for investors and become better investors. Women are twice[41] as likely to invest in women, too, which means that with more female investment, there'd be more women in leadership roles able to build more wealth and, therefore, end up as investors themselves. It's a domino effect. But more needs to be done.

We need more people from underrepresented backgrounds to finance these overlooked areas. They are the ones more likely to have the personal experience and understanding to want to back businesses that others overlook.

But that's difficult when we don't have a pile of money lying around, or we aren't born with business connections to help us get closer to the destination of becoming an investor. Therefore, we have to create it for ourselves. We have to build and scale a business that can't be ignored and has enough financial power that we can become investors.

What Needs to Change?

It is no secret that it's difficult for women and minorities to enter a historically male-dominated space with little diversity. They violate norms by being there, and history shows that women who don't 'behave' face more judgements and obstacles. I spoke to a (male) investor recently and asked him for his thoughts. With a 50/50 split in investing in male and female-led companies, I thought he'd have a more rounded view. In his experience, female founders do bring a better ROI, are more risk-aware and make better business decisions than his male investments. So, it would be fair to assume these traits would make us good investors, too.

But in his experience, he is approached far more often by men for investment than women and, therefore, the likelihood of investing in male-founded companies is higher. There are simply fewer women asking for funding and, as a result, fewer women accessing the knowledge and connections necessary to become investors themselves.

To create change, we need to change the status quo.

If we want a different outcome, we have to do something different. Just as Rosa Parks did when she refused to give up her seat on that bus in 1955. Or when Katherine Switzer entered the Boston Marathon in 1967 and broke the gender barrier for women in sport, we need people – women and men – to take a stand and change things. The obstacles women face will not go away without ongoing action and pressure to evolve. Changing the investment world and the business world will take time.

Countries all over the world are at different stages of evolution when it comes to these male-female issues, and some are more advanced than others when it comes to equality in finance. But who is better equipped to face these issues than women? The double standards, the judgements and the restrictions placed on girls and women mean we have no illusions about the challenges ahead of us. Even if we don't believe we can handle them, we can. Just think of all the crap we have to deal with just by existing.

We need more women with financial power. The more women who have power, the more likely we are to see increasing numbers of female-founded and female-led businesses succeed. When that happens, more women are likely to seek investment or to become investors, and we are more likely to see women in powerful roles.

It will become self-fulfilling.

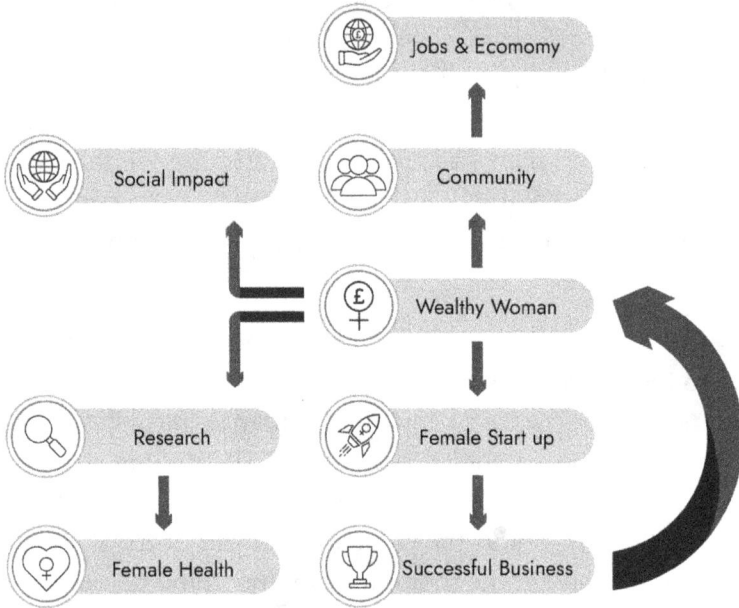

As I mentioned in Chapter 13, women are more likely to put their money towards creating a positive social impact, so wanting to have and earn more money is not a selfish thing. Women generally don't aim for the highest financial reward but rather for goals aligned with our values, or the values in our community or environment. When women have economic power, *everyone* benefits. We need power, not just for ourselves, but for our community, families and our collective futures.

This is simply a numbers game. That's all it is. The more we try, the more we fail, the more we have the data to figure out how to succeed.

And then we do.

15

HOW NOT TO FUCK IT UP

— How to Keep What You Earn —

So many women I talk to say, "I'm crap with money." But I don't believe that. They have just never been taught. Having to learn about this stuff and seek out financial education is not a reflection of women being bad at money; it's a reflection of how women have been left out of the conversation. It is a reflection of how badly systems have failed to provide the financial education we deserve and brought us up to believe that money was too complicated or 'not for women'.

Not anymore.

Most people are absolutely smart enough to understand this stuff, and if you've reached this chapter, you're one of them. You are creating the change. You have pushed past the confusion, overwhelm, possible boredom and definite frustration, and you're still here. Bloody brilliant. And bollocks to anyone who said you couldn't.

Now you're here, you'll be happy to learn that this final chapter doesn't contain more financial terminology; it's about what to do next. How to take all you've learned and use it to **keep** the money you have – or will have soon.

Every Upside Has a Downside

First, we have to acknowledge that knowing and understanding your numbers will create a strong foundation for your business. It will empower you to make the right decisions and come back from the wrong ones with confidence and resilience. (That bit is important.)

But there is an unexpected cost to knowing how to manage your money.

When it's going well, I've noticed that people tend to take their foot off the gas. Things start to drop off. Everyone gets a bit distracted. And that's when it all starts to unravel. We get complacent, and it's not just the business owners but the employees who do it, too, even at home with our personal finances. When things look good, details get overlooked. Nobody notices that things start heading towards a cliff...

Mistakes happen when things go well.

You can argue that we all make mistakes and we're only human. I agree, but as female business owners and entrepreneurs, we can't make the same mistakes as our male peers and expect the same treatment. Research has found that women and minorities are often punished more harshly for the same mistakes compared to others:[42] Harvard Business School[43] found that female financial advisors are 20% more likely to be fired for misconduct compared to men. They are also 30% less likely to find another job in the industry. If a female surgeon loses a patient, there is a 34% fall in future referrals. But there is no fallout when male surgeons lose a patient.

I have seen it in companies I've worked in: a senior female was accused of violating company policy by ringfencing revenue for herself. She was demoted, with all management responsibility stripped from her, her career and reputation tarnished. But a less senior male employee accused of misogynistic behaviour by several women, even to the point that a client refused to work with him, was simply given a mentor to *help* him work through his issues. He was later promoted. *His* career flourished.

If you violate a social norm, if you're too masculine, too ambitious, too outspoken in the pursuit of your goals, you are more likely to be penalised for your success and punished more harshly for your mistakes. My advice is to be even more focused when things are going well. We are, as humans, so motivated by the pressure of having to make things work that if you took that pressure away, would you have the same drive to succeed? Too much profit sitting in your bank as a safety net can kill your ambition and motivation. I think having a foot up your ass is a really good thing; a little discomfort can be a good motivator. Celebrate your successes. Absolutely. But use that as a sign to double down and spread your financial risk. If you have surplus profit in your business account, you have options:

1. Reinvestment

If things are going well, use your money to reinvest in an area of your business you'd like to grow. What areas of your business do you want to improve or that could use a cash boost? Invest in a new location or create an add-on service. Buy new equipment. What does your business need?

2. Take the money out

At one point, one of my clients had a million pounds of surplus cash that the business didn't need. They had a four-month reserve, which was more than enough, but they just couldn't decide what to do with it. They had no plans to sell and had no growth areas they wanted to invest in, so I told them their options:

- Put it in your pensions.
- Share it with your staff as a bonus.
- Buy an asset for the company.
- Look into a new revenue stream.

Do something with it, but don't just leave it sitting there. You will end up chipping away at it on pointless things or spending it all on something stupid.

3. Use it as an asset

There are some great ISAs and tax-efficient ways to get money out of your business, so take some wealth advice. It is not just for millionaires; if your business has a couple of hundred grand spare, talk to a wealth advisor. You could set up a trust fund for your children, make some wise investments, or explore pension options that work for you. Talk to an expert who can advise you on the best assets that will give you financial security.

🔨 If you are looking to sell, this is the only time I'd recommend leaving surplus cash in your business. It can be more tax-efficient to take surplus cash out as part of the exit deal than to take it out as dividends.

Your Money, Your Choice

What you do with your profits is a completely personal choice. If you want to buy a lodge in the woods and live off-grid, if you want to spend your golden years on a cruise rather than in a nursing home, each to their own. When Brass Tacks sold their business, Hannah treated herself to a Chanel bag she'd had her eye on for about twenty years. Then, she used the rest of the money to fund her lifestyle and retrain herself into a new career. If I had a massive chunk of change, I would probably buy myself something shiny and expensive, but most of it would go into investing for the kids' futures or into other assets to generate passive income. I would spread the money all over the place as a way of reducing my financial risk.

If you've started a business and you're running it well, do what makes you happy. Do not get distracted by what everyone else is doing with their money. You have done this to break free of the corporate shite. Don't crowbar yourself back into it or judge yourself for what you want to spend it on. Using your profits in this way just adds another layer of risk protection, which is way more valuable than holding cash. But you've worked hard for that money, so don't hoard it or blow it on something stupid. Do something useful with it.

How to Stay on Track

Building a successful business is not easy, yet it is rewarding. But the path to achieving that can be messy and filled with massive highs and horrible lows. It can be easy to get caught up in the day-to-day tasks and the drama of managing people, arguing with suppliers and clients, and you forget why you're doing it all. You go into survival mode: 'Gotta hit the numbers each month!' but you forget why or how you got there. For James and Michelle, running School Run Studio was difficult, operating in a constantly evolving landscape. It was difficult not to get distracted and compare themselves. For Brass Tacks, the most challenging period was Covid, and with Evergreen Assembly, they were constantly balancing their cashflow in an industry with high costs and even higher egos.

However, for all three businesses, keeping their eyes on the end goal kept them moving forward despite difficulties. You have to remind yourself what it's all for. When things get difficult, remember this:

$$G = FAB$$

Goals = Financials x Asking for help x Beliefs

Achieving your goals will be a result of how strong your financials are, your beliefs and your willingness to ask for help.

1. Goals

I know it's a really wanky thing to say, but it's important to keep reminding yourself why you're doing this and whether the decisions you're making are moving you in the right direction. Without a clear end goal:

- You don't have a clear business strategy.
- You won't know when you're drifting off course, away from your goals.
- You'll never know when you've 'made it' because you don't know what you're chasing.

A clear end goal is that magic number, that revenue you want to make, or the hours you have free to do whatever you want.

I understand that if there is a clear goal, there is also a fear of realising that you're failing. However, failure is actually a really good thing. It tells you that you messed it up and you need to bring it back in line. Then try the next thing. If you fail again, do it quickly. Bring it back in. Be laser-focused on what you're trying to achieve. Everyone goes off course. But unless you know how and where you've gone off course, you won't know how to bring yourself back.

So:

What is your goal?

What is your Magic Number?

What kind of business are you building and why?

2. Financials

This entire book is about understanding and managing your financial records. However, learning about it and actually doing it are completely different things. The realities of business often mean that our finances are the last thing we consider. That needs to change. Swap it around and ensure your finances are the first thing you check every week. To remind you, here are some things you must not forget to do:

- Track all costs. Set yourself up with some accounting software and track everything there.
- Check your P&L and how the numbers compare to your targets.
- Keep your cashflow healthy.
- Check your balance sheet regularly and make sure it's positive (or at least working towards it).
- Compare costs against your budget and adjust if needed.
- Revisit your forecasts often and keep them up to date.
- Make sure systems and processes are as efficient as possible.
- Benchmark against competitors.
- Stay as tax efficient as possible.
- Make sure you know how your personal and business finances interact with each other.

3. Ask for Help

Many women are more likely to keep persevering until they collapse rather than admit they need help. We prioritise our children, our husbands and our clients over our own aspirations. We tend to put ourselves on the back burner, which is just life. But if we want to achieve anything, we must have support. Not everyone has a supportive partner who shares caregiving responsibilities, but support doesn't necessarily have to come from a partner. It can come from a parent, a sibling, or a friendship group or network.

I have gained so much from various networks, even if it's just offloading my thoughts and asking for advice. Some of them are really narky and scratchy, and I don't like them at all. However, there are those where everyone is keen to share their time, energy and experiences. Having these connections is really important. Even if a network has nothing to do with running your business, having people to talk to and seek guidance from is essential. When I became a mum, having a network of other mums was incredible. If I hadn't had that,

I'd probably be in a hole in the ground right now. The same applies to business. Having a network of women who are experiencing similar challenges or who have already navigated them can be incredibly powerful. So, find them. You won't regret it.

> While you can have a network of male supporters, it's essential to connect with women who can understand your experiences. The business world is still very male-dominated, and building a network with those who share similar journeys is so important.

4. Beliefs

A lot of your potential is down to what you *think and believe* you can achieve. If you have money mindset or confidence issues, go and work on them, because nothing in the book will be useful to you if you don't act on it. I could give you all the information you need to build a multi-billion-dollar company, but if you don't think you deserve it or you lack the confidence to fight your corner, this won't work. You have to believe this is possible. The biggest pitfall I see is women holding themselves back, believing themselves unqualified or undeserving of their success and money. What if people judge you? What if you make a lot of money and people think you're greedy?

Who fucking cares? It is your business.

We are way less likely to say, "I want to build a twenty million pound business." Maybe we don't have the confidence to hit that bar or we don't think it's possible. Or we think it's crass that we have that financial goal, and people will judge us. But if that's what you want to do and it brings you the financial security you want, then do it. We will be judged whether we do or don't strive for something, so we might as well go for what we want. Research shows that women make excellent leaders[44] and are just as good as men at growing businesses. Why shouldn't we do it?

Welcome to Financial Independence

It would not be a bad thing to have more financially savvy women in the world. Women who know how to invest, grow their wealth through business or just budget with confidence. We don't all have to become business owners, but we do need to become financially educated. I don't care where you're from or what your background is, you are smart enough to learn this stuff, even if you have to go back and read this a second or third time, or message me on LinkedIn for more help. That doesn't mean you're any less intelligent. It means you're learning.

This is not rocket science, and there is no rule that says this has to be a stress-filled nightmare. You can make your path a lot smoother just by using what you've learned in this book. But be gentle on yourself. Question those moments you doubt yourself and what you're doing, because you are doing the right thing. I can't wrap my head around any scenario where this levelling out of financial education would be a bad thing for society. And anyone who suggests that more women with financial education would somehow take away from others is just bollocks.

Right now, there are certain groups of people who do have an advantage: they have more access to financial education. I totally get why they wouldn't want to give up their head start with money, or why they might see more women and minorities with more financial power as a threat. But I would argue that this isn't giving up their advantage; it's giving them more. More diversity of ideas, more brains, more innovation, more empathy and more equity. The only people who dislike diversity are those who benefit from keeping people divided and ignorant …

You may meet people who will question what you've learned in this book. They will disagree with what I've taught you and tell you something different. I have already had trolls on my LinkedIn page question my teachings, but only because they believe their way is the only way. Nothing I've taught you is incorrect, illegal or anything I would not advise clients to do. Fifteen years and hundreds of millions in profits for my clients should give you enough confidence in what you have learned. But make your own judgements. You are smart enough to know how to take what you've learned and use it. While there are absolutely some rules like tax and basic maths you have to stick to, there are other guidelines that you can adapt to your own situation. But only you can make that decision.

To finish, I want to say that I hope this book makes the whole idea of money and numbers slightly less terrifying for you. That you are more comfortable talking about it – and asking your questions. Even if this doesn't result in thousands of women starting businesses or turning into millionaires, that's ok, as long as we can all talk about money more openly, without shame or fear, because when we do, we can change the game. We can take up space, adjust the balance of power, and change who wins.

That spark of anger that pushed me towards writing this book began on a playing field that didn't have space for my daughter. It made me realise that the finance world doesn't make space for us either. But just because there is no space for us does not mean we can't play or have the potential to win. We should play the game anyway. It is time to own our own finances and become financial players with as much fearless knowledge, confidence and shame-free curiosity as anyone else.

Let's own our finances and change the game. See you on the field.

AUTHOR'S THOUGHTS

Writing this book has given me the opportunity to reflect on my work and things that have happened to me in my past. Although I come across as quite practical or laddish, I am really quite an emotional softie. I take a lot of things personally, and I worry all the time.

I carry with me a few scars from my work. Arguments, confrontations, and bad behaviour have left me feeling dented and bruised. I have been working in finance for twenty years – fifteen as an accountant – and I still have an ugly cry when these things happen.

But through writing this book, I've been able to reflect and realise that a lot of those scars and attacks weren't my fault. I have been able to let go of some things I took very personally.

I want to be clear that nothing excuses bad behaviour. No one deserves to be bullied or demeaned for doing their job, but after writing this book, I can understand that bad behaviour a little better.

I have always been good at translating financial jargon, but that wasn't enough to make a good book. I have had to question the crux of why people don't understand money and why they're scared of it. It has made me dive deeper into my role as a CFO more than ever before, and it has helped me recognise that bad behaviour often comes from fear and frustration. For people who feel they *should* understand this stuff, it can be frightening to lose their sense of control. Of course, they snap. But that's not a reflection on me.

And, yes, maybe sometimes I am a bit too defensive. As an accountant, you assume you are taught everything you need to know, but there are many things I didn't know. I didn't know people had these gaps in their knowledge, and I've had to completely reframe ideas, think more deeply about how to simplify them and how to put them into the right words. It has made me more sympathetic to how challenging this subject can be, and I'm more motivated to encourage people to ask the questions they need to ask, without shame or embarrassment.

For the last fifteen years, all I've worked with is numbers. Writing this book has been a true learning experience. It has been terrifying to try something completely out of my comfort zone, but I know it has made me a better CFO and business advisor. I understand what I do, and what my clients need from me, on a much deeper level. It feels good. What started as a simple desire to help more women with their money, in a way, has come full circle and helped me, too.

So, thank you.

ACKNOWLEDGEMENTS AND THANKS

This book would not exist without the people who have supported, challenged and inspired me over the years.

To my husband, you are so much more than my partner in life. You are my equal, my teammate, my anchor (not wanker!). You support me even when I don't realise I need it. You have never once doubted, dismissed or ridiculed my ambitions, even when I doubted myself. Thank you for walking beside me with strength, humour and endless love. I couldn't have done this, or so many other things, without you.

To my children, who remind me daily why building something with purpose matters and why we should never bend or change ourselves to fit. You are my greatest motivation and proudest accomplishment. Thank you for inspiring me to make even a tiny ripple in the world and pave a better future for you to live in.

To Corinna, thank you for persevering through something so out of your comfort zone, for pushing me to explain things more clearly and for helping me become a better CFO in the process. You brought clarity, patience and structure to the chaos in my head, and you did it while tolerating my rants and my swearing! Without you, this would still be just a collection of thoughts in my brain.

To the women who've shaped my career: Shirley, my first ever boss, who showed me patience and kindness when I needed it most. Thank you for teaching me that leadership begins with compassion. Xenia, whose high standards and relentless drive pushed me to raise my own. You made me sharper, stronger and more prepared. Emma, who inspired me to seek meaning in my work. Your passion lit a fire in me that still burns.

To a group of Loud Women who gave me a seat at their table, shared ideas and resources, supported and encouraged me through the final stages of this process and the whole of the journey to building my own business.

To the countless women I've had the privilege to work with over the past fifteen years, your ambition, resilience and brilliance are the reasons this book was written. You are building more than businesses; you are shaping futures. I am honoured to be part of your journey.

And finally, to you, my reader. Thank you for picking up this book and investing in yourself. I hope what's inside helps you feel more confident, more equipped and more powerful in building the businesses (and life) you deserve.

ABOUT THE AUTHOR

Laura Linden is a fractional CFO and financial strategist. As the founder of Feisty FD (https://www.feistyfd.com/), she teaches business owners how not to fuck up their finances. Through the Feisty FD educational platform, she provides clarity and comfort for business owners who want to build resilient businesses. Laura has worked in finance since 2002 and helped a variety of businesses scale, secure funding and successfully exit, from recruitment companies to independent service providers to multi-nationals. Her approach is simple: no jargon, no lectures, just straight-talking strategies that help women understand their finances, build resilience, and take control of their financial future. Laura believes that knowing your numbers isn't about maths, it's about freedom.

She lives in Surrey with her husband, two children and two rescue dogs. When she's not helping businesses grow, you can find her in the kitchen singing power ballads into a ladle, or reading fantasy novels (guilty pleasure, don't judge!).

You can reach Laura at:

✉ Email – laura@feistyfd.com
🅵 Facebook – <u>facebook.com/laura.linden.feistyfd</u>
🅾 Instagram – <u>instagram.com/feistyfd</u>
🅸🅽 LinkedIn – <u>linkedin.com/in/laura-linden-feisty</u>
🌐 Website – <u>www.feistyfd.com</u>

ENDNOTES/ REFERENCES

1. https://www.british-business-bank.co.uk/sites/g/files/sovrnj166/files/2022-11/UK_VC_and_Female_Founders_Report_British_Business_Bank.pdf

2. https://assets.publishing.service.gov.uk/media/5c8147e2e5274a2a595bb24a/RoseReview_Digital_FINAL.PDF

3. https://ourworld.unu.edu/en/everyone-benefits-from-more-women-in-power

4. Invisible Women p71

5. https://www.investinwomentaskforce.org/

6. https://www.kleinworthambros.com/fileadmin/user_upload/kleinworthambros/pdf/The_WealthiHer_Network_Report_2019.pdf

7. https://www.forbes.com/sites/shelleyzalis/2024/09/10/the-feminization-of-wealth-rewriting-the-narrative-for-women-investors/

8. https://www.mckinsey.com/industries/financial-services/our-insights/the-new-face-of-wealth-the-rise-of-the-female-investor

9. https://www.forbes.com/councils/
forbesbusinesscouncil/2024/11/18/the-great-wealth-transfer-an-84-
trillion-investment-opportunity-for-women/

10. https://www.forbes.com/councils/
forbesbusinesscouncil/2024/11/18/the-great-wealth-transfer-an-84-
trillion-investment-opportunity-for-women/

11. https://www.mckinsey.com/industries/
financial-services/our-insights/the-new-face-of-wealth-the-rise-of-
the-female-investor

12. https://www.ubs.com/global/en/media/display-
page-ndp/en-20190306-study-reveals-multi-generational-problem.
html

13. https://www.forbes.com/lists/power-women/

14. https://www.forbes.com/profile/mackenzie-scott/

15. https://inews.co.uk/inews-lifestyle/what-worlds-richest-
men-learn-worlds-richest-women-3518490

16. https://www.enterpriseresearch.ac.uk/wp-content/
uploads/2024/07/12828-%E2%80%A2-GEM-UK-23-24-WEB-
READY-22.07.24.pdf

17. Operating Profit is similar to EBIT: Earnings Before
Interest and Tax.

18. https://10years.firstround.com/

19. https://www.weforum.org/stories/2023/06/women-
entrepreneurs-frontier-markets-opportunity/

20. https://www.enterprise.cam.ac.uk/women-equity-and-
venture-capital/

21. https://www.forbes.com/sites/kimelsesser/2022/04/29/
women-arent-risk-averse-they-just-face-consequences-when-they-
take-risks/

22. https://leadershipcircle.com/wp-content/ uploads/2022/03/Research-on-Female-and-Male-Leaders-White-Paper-2022-03-17.pdf

23. Rose Review pg 54

24. https://www.cbs.dk/en/cbs-agenda/areas/news/female-entrepreneurs-face-discrimination-from-their-own-employees

25. https://onlinelibrary.wiley.com/doi/abs/10.1111/ jasp.12702

26. Rose Review P10

27. https://www.natwestgroup.com/news-and-insights/ news-room/press-releases/enterprise/2024/feb/record-900000-new-companies-launched-in-2023.html

28. Alison Rose Review p7

29. https://www.institutionalinvestor.com/ article/2bstpo0h7569w26cav400/culture/women-are-more-likely-to-back-impact-investments-than-men-heres-why

30. Pledging to commit their 30 percent equity in the company to philanthropic endeavours

31. https://www.forbes.com/sites/anafaguy/2024/02/26/ widow-of-billionaire-david-gottesman-donates-1-billion-for-free-medical-school-tuition/

32. https://www.bbc.co.uk/news/articles/c3vk3440ze9o

33. https://www.billboard.com/lists/ taylor-swifts-charity-donations-gifts-timeline/nov-2023-she-supports-the-mahomies-foundation/

34. https://www.forbes.com/sites/ elizabethedwards/2021/02/24/check-your-stats-the-lack-of-diversity-in-venture-capital-is-worse-than-it-looks/

35. https://sifted.eu/articles/even-in-femtech-it-still-pays-to-be-a-male-founder

36. https://www.weforum.org/stories/2023/12/how-we-can-close-the-venture-capital-gender-gap/

37. https://www.ifc.org/content/dam/ifc/doc/mgrt/exec-summary-moving-toward-gender-balance-final.pdf

38. https://eif4smes.medium.com/vc-factor-gender-lens-b8a9b2df14a7

39. https://nvca.org/press_releases/new-survey-reflects-lack-women-minorities-senior-investment-roles-venture-capital-firms/

40. https://leadershipcircle.com/wp-content/uploads/2022/03/Research-on-Female-and-Male-Leaders-White-Paper-2022-03-17.pdf

41. https://www.kauffmanfellows.org/journal/women-vcs-invest-in-up-to-2x-more-female-founders

42. https://www.weforum.org/stories/2019/06/the-punishment-gap-how-workplace-mistakes-hurt-women-and-minorities-most/

43. Egan, Mark, Gregor Matvos, and Amit Seru. "When Harry Fired Sally: The Double Standard in Punishing Misconduct." Journal of Political Economy 130, no. 5 (May 2022): 1184–1248. https://www.hbs.edu/faculty/Pages/item.aspx?num=60114

44. https://www.forbes.com/sites/kevinkruse/2023/03/31/new-research-women-more-effective-than-men-in-all-leadership-measures/